Stephen Wehrmann, DVM

Lhasa Apsos

Everything about Purchase, Care,
Nutrition, Breeding, and Diseases

With a Special Chapter on
Understanding Lhasa Apsos

With 24 Color Photographs
and 33 Drawings

Consulting Editor: Matthew M. Vriends, PhD

BARRON'S

About the Author:
Stephen Wehrmann is a veterinarian practicing in St. Petersburg, Florida. After graduating from the University of Hawaii with a B.A. in zoology, he received his doctorate of veterinary medicine from the University of Missouri. A frequent lecturer to pet groups, Dr. Wehrmann has also authored many articles regarding companion animal care that have appeared in regional and national publications.

All inquiries should be addressed to:
Barron's Educational Series, Inc.
250 Wireless Boulevard
Hauppauge, NY 11788

Library of Congress Catalog Card No. 89-38540

International Standard Book No. 0-8120-3950-5

Library of Congress Cataloging in Publication Data

Wehrmann, Stephen.
    Lhasa apsos : everything about purchase, care nutrition, breeding, and diseases : with a special chapter on understanding lhasa apsos / Stephen Wehrmann : with color photographs by well-known photographers and drawings by Michele Earle-Bridges ; consulting editor, Matthew M. Vriends.
        p.   cm.
    ISBN 0-8120-3950-5
    1. Lhasa apsos. I.   Vriends, Matthew M., 1937–   . II. Title.
SF429.L5W44   1990
636.7′2—dc20   89-38540
                                        CIP

Printed and Bound in Hong Kong

20 19 18 17 16 15 14 13 12 11 10

Photo Credits:
Eugene Butenas, LCA Photography: pages 45, 46, 63 bottom left; back cover. Robert Lauwers, RLP Media: pages 10, 27, 28, 63 bottom right; back cover. William van Vught: front cover, inside front cover; pages 9, 63 top, 64; back cover.

Illustrations:
Michele Earle-Bridges

Advice and Warning:
This book is concerned with selecting, keeping, and raising Lhasa apsos. The publisher and the author think it is important to point out that the advice and information for Lhasa apso maintenance applies to healthy, normally developed animals. Anyone who acquires an adult dog or one from an animal shelter must consider that the animal may have behavioral problems and may, for example, bite without any visible provocation. Such anxiety-biters are dangerous for the owner as well as the general public.

Caution is further advised in the association of children with dogs, in meetings with other dogs, and in exercising the dog without a leash.

Contents

Contents

Preface

"Man's best friend" has appropriately described our relationship with dogs for a long time. As a veterinarian, I've had the opportunity and privilege to observe the special bond that develops between a dog and its owner. I have talked to all sorts of people in all walks of life about their dogs. And believe me, everybody loves to talk about their dog! Lhasa apso owners are no exception. The Lhasa apso is a faithful companion dog that serves its master or mistress with dedication and loyalty. Originating on the high plateau of Tibet, Lhasa apsos were bred to be guard dogs of aristocratic households. In the Tibetan language the Lhasa is called "Abso Seng Kye" which means "barking sentinel lion dog"—an appropriate name indeed! Lhasa owners have consistently told me that their Lhasa apso is the best watch dog they have ever had. Lhasas are hardy little dogs, capable of thriving in almost any climate and environment. They are well suited and content to be indoor dogs, bringing a complimentary mixture of companionship and watchfulness to their respective households.

In this book, I have attempted to provide a complete overview of the essentials of owning and caring for a Lhasa apso. I hope this book will stimulate you to learn as much as you can about your Lhasa, because the more you know about your pet the better your relationship will be. Throughout the book, I have answered questions Lhasa owners have asked me most frequently. I have tried to present the material in a straightforward, practical manner, providing useful information that you can refer to whenever you have a question about your Lhasa apso. Although it is not possible to answer every conceivable question that might arise, I hope this book will help steer you in the right direction. The tips and suggestions about caring for your Lhasa are based on years of experience and a warehouse of knowledge from breeders, Lhasa owners, and veterinarians.

Owning and caring for a Lhasa apso, or any dog for that matter, is a tremendous responsibility. Your Lhasa will depend on you for almost everything. However, the rewards are great for the effort put forward. The love and attention you give your Lhasa will be returned to you many times over.

In preparing this book, I would like to thank Dr. Matthew Vriends for his generous support and unwavering enthusiasm during the entire project. I also want to extend my sincere appreciation to John Mandeville, Director of Judging, Research and Development of the American Kennel Club, who read the manuscript and made many astute suggestions that have enabled me to increase the usefulness of this pet owner's manual. Sincere thanks also go to Kris Schmitz for her invaluable assistance in preparation of the text and to Michele Earl-Bridges for her excellent illustrations throughout the book. I also wish to express gratitude to my colleagues Drs. Robert Hunt and Leon Sellers and to the entire staff at Bayshore Animal Hospital for their encouraging words and helpful suggestions. Lastly, I would like to thank all of the Lhasa apso owners and breeders who shared their knowledge and insights with me.

Considerations Before You Buy

Dogs have occupied a special place in the hearts of human beings for thousands of years. We receive unconditional love and affection from our canine friends. They don't care who we are or what we look like. Just give them healthy doses of affection, kindness, and guidance, and they will reward us with years of loyal companionship. Scientists have begun to recognize that pets can give us emotional support and improve our well-being. Studies have shown people are more relaxed, smile more, and are less likely to have elevated blood pressure in the presence of pets. Of course, anybody who has owned a dog knows this already!

Lhasa apsos are a popular breed with my clients. As a veterinarian, I observe first hand the interactions between Lhasas and their owners. Lhasas quickly become members of the family. It is very rewarding to see a family bring in a new Lhasa puppy for its first examination and watch the bond develop between them over the years.

Before rushing out to purchase your new Lhasa apso, sit down with your family and carefully consider all the responsibilities of owning a dog. Many Lhasa apsos live to be 15 years old or more, so acquiring one is a long-term commitment. Are you willing to take time out of your schedule every day to spend with your dog? Be realistic about who will be taking care of your Lhasa on a day-to-day basis. I've never met a child who wouldn't like to have a puppy. However, once the novelty has worn off, Mom or Dad must usually shoulder the responsibility for feeding, watering, and exercising. Frequent brushing and grooming are also essential. The Lhasa's long, thick coat becomes easily matted if neglected.

Financial obligations should be clearly understood. The initial cost of a Lhasa is only a small part of the total amount of money you will spend on your pet during his or her lifetime. Your Lhasa will need vaccinations and routine checkups by your veterinarian. Additional veterinary services will be needed in the event your Lhasa becomes ill or has an accident. There will be expenses for grooming. You can pay a professional groomer or purchase brushes, clipper scissors, shampoos, etc., and do the job at home. When you are away from home and can't take your Lhasa with you, boarding fees will be incurred. Fortunately, because of their small size, the day-to-day feed cost of owning Lhasas is relatively small.

Is a Lhasa Apso Right for You?

Why choose a Lhasa apso? There are many reasons Lhasas are popular household pets. Their comparatively small size makes them ideal for people who want an indoor dog or just don't have the room or yard that a larger dog needs. Each breed has its own space and exercise requirements. It would not be fair for a large, active dog such as an Irish setter or German shepherd to be cooped up

The Lhasa Apso, native to Tibet, is known as *Apso Seng Kye*—"barking sentinel lion dog." Inquisitive and alert, the Lhasa will notify its owner of approaching visitors.

in an apartment all day long with little chance for exercise. Neurotic and destructive habits usually develop under these conditions. However, a Lhasa apso can prosper in a relatively confined environment with limited exercise. A daily walk on a leash or a romp in the yard will keep them in good spirits and maintain physical fitness. Lhasas are generally content to be guardians of the castle. By their nature and breeding, they are excellent watch dogs. Their alertness and ability to distinguish friend from foe are keenly developed traits dating back hundreds of years to when they were sentinel dogs for the imperial families of Tibet and China.

Well-bred Lhasas should have an even, good-natured temperament. They thrive on human contact and enjoy being considered part of the family, although they tend to be standoffish and wary of strangers. Some Lhasas can become aggressive, strong-willed, and may try to dominate the household. This reflects poor breeding and improper training. Therefore, be very wary of breeders who do not select for desirable personality traits (see pages 11–12).

Plan on spending at least one hour per week washing and grooming your Lhasa. If you start when your Lhasa is a young puppy, grooming will develop into an emotionally satisfying experience for you and your pet. Your Lhasa will eagerly look forward to the grooming sessions. From time to time, you may elect to take your Lhasa to a professional groomer for styling, dipping, and bathing. Since Lhasas have long, thick coats that become easily matted, you may decide to keep your pet clipped for easier care.

To sum up, Lhasa apsos are one of the most popular breeds in my veterinary practice. They are hardy, alert, and adapt well to modern urban lifestyles. They are loved by families with children and elderly retirees alike. They can be easily carried and are happy to be confined indoors. Despite their small size and teddy-bear appearance, they are dedicated, loyal guardians of the household.

Puppy or Mature Dog?

Whether you choose to raise a puppy or adopt an adult dog will depend on your own personal preferences and situation at home. There is immense joy and satisfaction gained from raising a puppy and watching it grow into adulthood. Puppies are fun and bring out the best in all of us. Their boundless energy and unbridled enthusiasm make them irresistible and people become attached to them very quickly. The bond that develops between the puppy and its owner lays the foundation for a rewarding, lifelong relationship. The main advantage of a puppy is that you are starting with a "blank slate." The puppy will adapt to your family and will grow to accept the rules of your house. Puppies will naturally accept children and develop a strong bond with them. However, it is important to instruct children on how to treat their new puppy (see page 15). Remember, it is much easier to train a puppy than to retrain an adult dog that has learned bad habits.

Bear in mind, however, that raising a puppy requires lots of time and patience on your part. Housebreaking, feeding schedules, do's and don'ts all have to be learned and reinforced. This requires patience and persistence. In addition, you can never be totally sure of what kind of personality a puppy will have as an adult.

An adult dog, on the other hand, has a well-developed personality, so you know what you're getting. With an adult dog you will also know exactly what the markings, color, and size will be. This could be important if you plan to show or breed your Lhasa. Some people prefer a mature dog, if it is well trained, because they don't have to go through the rigors of housebreaking, training, and finding their favorite slippers chewed into several pieces!

However, I would be very cautious before adopting an adult dog. Many times people give up their dog because of some undesirable trait. The dog may be difficult to train or housebreak, aggressive toward people or other animals, or have a

Considerations Before You Buy

serious medical problem. Get a complete history of the dog so there won't be any surprises down the road. It can sometimes be difficult for an adult dog to adjust, particularly if there are children or other animals in the new household.

Male or Female?

Your choice of a male or female Lhasa depends on your own personality and reasons for owning a dog. If you desire to breed your Lhasa the choice is easy—you'll want a female. Females are smaller than males and are generally more loving and gentle. Because of their gentle nature, females tend to be recommended for families with children. Males tend to be more dominant and assertive. In fact, they may openly challenge you and try to become the dominant member of the household. Males that are strong-willed require more training and discipline. Unless you plan to use your Lhasa for a stud dog, I strongly recommend neutering him at six months of age. He will be less likely to roam or fight and more content to let you be master of the house. Don't worry about his losing his loyalty or sentinel instincts. A neutered male is simply more even-tempered and easily managed.

If you choose a female and elect not to breed her, have her spayed (ovariohysterectomy) when she is 6 to 12 months old. Most females will have their first heat during this period. They usually come into season approximately every six months after their first heat. The heat period, which is characterized by blood-tinged vaginal discharge, lasts about two weeks (see page 55). During this time your house will be besieged by every male suitor in the neighborhood and beyond! You will quickly find out how strong the breeding instinct is in dogs. Clients have told me male dogs have scaled ten-foot fences in search of a romantic interlude with a female in season!

Where to Obtain Your Dog

Once you have decided what kind of Lhasa apso you want—puppy or adult dog, male or female, pet or show quality—the fun part really begins! The search for your canine companion should include exciting trips to local breeders, dog shows, and pet stores. Remember, shop around and try to resist latching on to the first cute Lhasa you find.

Pet Stores and Pet Departments

Pet stores can be an attractive place to purchase a puppy. However, all pet stores are not created equal; wide variations exist regarding quality of puppies, the personnel's knowledge of the breed, and the services offered. Certainly a sturdy, good-quality, healthy puppy can be obtained at a pet store; but the key factor is the pet store's source of puppies. Some pet stores and pet departments of larger stores obtain quality puppies from first-rate breeders; others purchase substandard, genetically inferior livestock from large "puppy mills." These puppy mills mass-produce puppies with little regard for the integrity and long-term soundness of the breed. Keep in mind that nobody can guarantee exactly what a puppy will turn out to be like as an adult; but the more information you can obtain about a puppy's dam and sire, the better. Choose pet stores that have good reputations and maintain clean and cheerful environments for their animals.

In their native land of Tibet, it was considered a great honor to receive a Lhasa apso as a gift. These noble, hardy little dogs are known for their long dense coats and unwavering loyalty to their owners. Two beautifully groomed Lhasas with coats of contrasting colors are shown. Above: tan with touches of light gold and black; below: an almost solid black.

Considerations Before You Buy

Professional and Amateur Breeders

Breeders can be a reliable source of Lhasas that are consistently healthy and of high quality. Local breeders can be found in the classified section of your newspaper or you can contact the local kennel Club in your area for a more comprehensive list of breeders in your vicinity and elsewhere. Your veterinarian may be able to help. In my animal hospital I have a breeder catalog that is popular with clients because I know many of the breeders personally.

Reputable breeders will encourage you to ask lots of questions and will be happy to show you their facilities. Small breeders may not have any facilities! Their breeding stock may be their own family pets. In fact, breeding dogs is more of a hobby and labor of love than a business for many small breeders. They generally shower their puppies with lots of love and attention, resulting in well-socialized puppies at adoption time (around eight weeks of age). Conscientious breeders are concerned about placing their puppies in caring, responsible homes. They may even ask you some questions about your future plans for the puppy and the kind of home life the puppy will be given.

Here are some important questions to consider when visiting the breeder. Is the environment clean and relatively odor-free? Do the breeders show genuine concern for the animals? Are the dogs groomed and well cared for with no major flea and tick problems?

One big advantage of buying your Lhasa puppy from a breeder is that you can see the littermates, the mother, and sometimes even the father. This will give you a better idea of what you can expect your puppy to look and act like as an adult. Due to whelping, nursing, and raising a litter, the mother may not be in top form. Her coat may be dull and she may look slightly thin. Nonetheless, she should appear healthy and exhibit the kind of disposition you are looking for.

Selecting a Puppy—What to Look for

The first rule in selecting a puppy is *take your time*. Don't rush into things and don't buy impulsively. It is very easy to fall in love with the first puppy you see. I have met many people who have purchased a puppy at a pet store because they "felt sorry for it" or "it was cute," only to discover they later had to give up the dog because of unrealistic expectations or a serious medical or behavioral flaw.

Do you want a top-notch show dog for breeding and entering in dog shows or are you primarily interested in a Lhasa as a companion and household pet? A show dog must conform to certain breed standards (see page 68), such as height, conformation, and character. A pet-quality Lhasa may exhibit minor flaws in regard to these breed standards. If the breeding has been sound, these imperfections are usually so subtle that they may be detectable only by the trained eye of a breeder or show judge. Such minor imperfections should in no way diminish a pet—quality purebred Lhasa's health, disposition, or value as a loving member of the family.

If you have decided that you want a show dog, be prepared to pay considerably more than you would for a pet-quality Lhasa. Also, keep in mind that even though the parents may be champion show dogs, there is no guarantee the puppy will turn out to be the same way.

Whether you are purchasing at a pet store or from a breeder, it is a good idea to visit a litter of puppies you are interested in more than once. First

Above: Lhasas adapt quite nicely to indoor living; they are ideal pets for apartment dwellers. Below: Two or more Lhasas will enjoy each other's company both indoors and outdoors.

impressions are not always accurate. On one visit the puppies may appear sleepy and sluggish; on the next, they may be active and playful. This could be because the puppies had just eaten before the first visit. Generally you won't glean too much useful information about characteristics of the individual puppies until they are at least six weeks old. I wouldn't recommend committing to a particular puppy until the litter is about eight weeks old. By then their personalities will be more clearly developed. Puppies should not be adopted and removed from the litter until they are at least six to eight weeks old. This allows proper socialization to take place between littermates and their mother.

Take plenty of time to observe the puppies' behavior—first at a distance, then up close. Watch the puppies interact with each other. Their different personalities will begin to emerge. Playful, alert, inquisitive puppies are desirable. Avoid domineering and overly assertive puppies. As adults they may challenge your authority and be difficult to train and discipline. A very timid puppy that with-

Be gentle when handling a young puppy. Always support the back by placing a hand underneath the hindquarters.

draws from the litter and avoids interaction may turn out to be a very shy dog that lacks enthusiasm.

Healthy puppies should have glossy coats and be in good flesh. Pick them up and examine them closely. The eyes should be clear and bright with no discharge. The nose should be cool and moist but not runny. Check the mouth. Pink gums are a sign of good health. If the gums are pale the puppies may have worms, fleas, or other more serious diseases. A slightly undershot bite, meaning the lower jaw protrudes from the mouth, is normal for Lhasa apsos. The area around the anus should not be soiled or emit a foul odor. If it does, the puppy may be suffering from diarrhea.

Pedigree and Registration

Before making a final decision and completing the sale, make sure the puppy's health records, pedigree, and registration papers are in order. A puppy should have a health certificate signed by a veterinarian stating the puppy has been examined. Dates of vaccination and deworming should also be stated. Your veterinarian can then set up a vaccination schedule based on this information.

A pedigree is not an official document. It is merely a chart showing the ancestral tree of the puppy. A pedigree is prepared by the breeder, stating the dam and sire and past relatives. A pedigree does not guarantee that the dog is registered with the American Kennel Club.

The American Kennel Club (AKC) registration certificate is an official document stating that your Lhasa apso is purebred. You should receive application papers from the breeder to register the puppy in your name. Once you choose a name for the puppy complete the application form and mail it to the AKC address on the application with the appropriate filing fee. You will then receive a certificate of registration from the AKC.

Your New Dog at Home

This chapter will be devoted to getting you and your new Lhasa started on the right track. Dogs tend to be creatures of habit, therefore any change in their daily routine or environment is potentially stressful to them. With a little advance preparation and some tips about what to expect from your new family member, the transition from your Lhasa's previous home to yours will be smooth and stress to you and your new Lhasa will be minimal. I say minimal, because don't expect everything to go perfectly the first few days your new Lhasa is home with you. Whether you are bringing home a puppy or an adult dog there will be a period of adjustment of a few days to get your pet settled in and comfortable.

This "settling in" period is very important. The tone for you and your Lhasa's relationship is established during this time. The satisfying lifelong bond that we feel for our pets starts from the day they enter our home, so get them started out on the right foot! As you teach your Lhasa about proper behavior, feeding, and sleeping arrangements, remember—patience and consistency will be your two most valuable virtues.

Preparing for Your New Arrival— Making Your Home Safe

It is a good idea to prepare your house and yard *before* bringing the new puppy home because once the puppy arrives everyone will be caught up in all the excitement of the new housemate.

First of all, make sure your house and yard are as safe as they can be for the new arrival. Puppies are naturally inquisitive and there is practically nothing they won't chew on. Check the carpets and furniture for sewing needles, thimbles, balls, etc., and remove anything that is small enough for the puppy to swallow. If these items are ingested, they may cause perforations or obstructions of the stomach and intestines. At my animal hospital we have a collection of items ranging from needles and fish hooks to rubber balls, corn cobs, and plastic caps

that we have had to remove surgically from dogs' stomachs or intestines. Most of these accidents could have been prevented. Be sure all potentially harmful substances are well out of reach. This includes rat poison, roach baits, insecticides, and caustic agents such as bleach and detergents. Keep electric cords away from the puppy. I have seen severe burns in puppies' mouths from chewing live, hot wires. Any personal valuables or fragile items within the puppy's reach should be moved. A torn sock or slipper is one thing but a damaged family heirloom may not be appreciated!

Some common ornamental plants are hazardous to your Lhasa if they are accidently chewed or ingested. Take an inventory of your house plants and make sure they aren't potentially toxic. As I have reiterated before, everything is fair game when it comes to a puppy's curiosity and desire to chew. Some of the common ornamental plants that are potentially toxic include: philodendron, dieffenbachia, poinsettia, oleander, wisteria, larkspur, jasmine, and lily of the valley, to name a few.

A fenced-in yard provides an excellent place for exercise without constant supervision.

Your New Dog at Home

This is by no means the entire list of toxic plants There are just too many to list here. If there are any doubts in your mind about a particular plant be sure to move it to an inaccessible location away from your puppy. Call your veterinarian or poison-control center for specific questions regarding ornamental or household plants.

As for the yard or garage, or wherever your puppy will be allowed to snoop around, inspect the premises and remove anything that might be dangerous to your pet. Oils, paints, pesticides, herbicides, etc., should all be put away safely. Antifreeze is very toxic to pets; a few laps of it can kill them. It's especially dangerous because antifreeze has a sweet taste and dogs will drink it. Basically, try to anticipate potential accidents before they happen!

Taking Your Puppy Home—Getting Settled

The joyous occasion you have been anticipating has finally arrived. You have brought your new Lhasa puppy home. Your puppy may seem a bit shy and reserved at first. He or she may be exhibiting separation anxiety. You would be anxious too if you had just left the security of your mother and littermates. Initially your home is a strange new environment for the puppy. Fortunately it does not take very long for them to get over their apprehension. Your puppy will adapt quickly. All it takes are generous doses of affection and reassurance for him or her to feel right at home.

Begin training your puppy as soon as you arrive at home. If it's been a fairly long ride in the car the puppy may need to eliminate. Take him out in the yard to an area where you desire him to eliminate regularly. Praise him if he performs. This will mark his area for future reference and he will return to the familiar territory. When your puppy enters his new home, he will want to do some exploring. Under constant supervision, let him meander around the house in the areas where he will be allowed.

For the first three or four days he is home with you it is a good idea to maintain the same diet and feeding schedule the puppy has been accustomed to. If you then wish to change the puppy's diet and schedule, do so gradually over a five- to seven-day period. Start by mixing a small amount of the new dog food with his old food. Each day increase the percentage of the new food in the mixture until you have completely converted your puppy over to his new ration. This will help reduce the possibility of your Lhasa developing diarrhea due to abrupt changes in diet. For more detailed feeding instructions refer to Chapter 5, "Feeding Puppies."

The Den—Security and Comfort

When it gets a little hectic around the house and your puppy is worn out from all the attention he has been getting, or it's simply time to bed down for the night, your Lhasa will want a place he can call his own—a refuge that offers security and comfort. Your puppy's needs will be satisfied in this regard by providing him or her with a den. In the wild, a puppy's den would be a cave, hollow log, or other small confined area where he and his littermates could rest and feel safe and secure. In your house a den could be a box, a basket, or a metal or wooden crate. Plastic traveling carriers used by airlines work well also. Initially, the den should be constructed so the puppy can't get out and should be covered. It shouldn't be too large. The den should be big enough for the puppy to stand up, turn around, stretch out, and have plenty of room to sleep comfortably. All these things will help retain the coziness and security a den provides for a puppy. Don't fall into the trap of thinking the den is a cage or prison for your puppy. Quite the contrary. Once the puppy gets used to it, he will consider it a sanctuary from all the activities of the house, a place where he or she can retire in peace.

Your New Dog at Home

There are other advantages to establishing a den. Under most circumstances a puppy's instinct is not to soil its own den. This can be a great aid in housebreaking a puppy. While you are away from home for short periods of time, placing your puppy in his den will prevent him from getting into any mischief. Also, if your pet's den is a crate or carrier, you can take it with you when traveling. It is very reassuring to your Lhasa to have something familiar in a strange environment. There is nothing like a "home away from home" from your pet's point of view.

How do you accustom your puppy to his new den? You can start using the den the first day the puppy is home with you. A young puppy will take several naps during the day with intervals of play in between. Place the puppy in the den during his naps. If he sleeps in the den during the day it will be more familiar to him at night for bedtime. To make the den comfortable and reassuring to the puppy put towels or old clothing with your scent inside. Don't put food or water inside the den, as they will be spilled and make a mess.

At first, when your puppy is young and can't go all night without eliminating, place the den in a small area such as a bathroom or laundry room. Lay some papers out and leave the door of the den open. That way if the puppy needs to eliminate at 4:00 A.M. he or she may do so outside the den, and you can get a good night's sleep without feeling guilty about letting him go out!

One word of caution—expect your Lhasa to whine, whimper, and cry the first couple of nights in the den or crate. Even though you'll be tempted—don't give in. In the long run, getting your puppy accustomed to its den is doing both you and your puppy a favor. If, initially, he has difficulty falling asleep, you may place a warm water bottle wrapped in a towel inside the den or a ticking alarm clock outside the den. This may reassure your puppy by simulating its mother's and littermates' warmth and heartbeat.

The den should not be a daylong babysitter for your Lhasa. Don't leave your pet in the crate for more than three or four hours except at night when it's sleeping. Try to keep your Lhasa's association with the den a positive one.

Children and Lhasas

Nothing delights children more than presenting them with a new puppy. A deep mutual affection quickly develops between the youngsters. Lhasa puppies make good, loyal companions for children.

It is very important for parents to instruct their children how to properly handle and care for their new dog. Children should be made aware their new pet has needs and feelings that should be respected. Of course, the amount of unsupervised interaction and responsibilities given to children depends on their ages. Toddlers and pre-school age children require especially close supervision. They need to be taught how not to harm the puppy inadvertently.

Paper training your Lhasa puppy may be necessary if he or she must be left unattended for several hours during the day.

Your New Dog at Home

Older children can assume some of the primary care—i.e., feeding, watering, bathing, and taking the dog for a walk. These daily activities need to be monitored closely by an adult to make sure the dog is not being neglected. Certain aspects of your Lhasa's care needs to be assumed by a responsible adult. This includes medical care, establishing a proper diet, and obedience training. By all means involve your children in caring for your Lhasa. It will teach them how to be responsible and will strengthen the bond between the children and their pet.

Adjusting To Other Pets

New puppies usually get along fine with other pets, whether it be cats or dogs. Puppies are naturally submissive to other animals and therefore the established order of the house is not upset. However, your other pets may become slightly annoyed because of the new Lhasa's boundless energy and constant desire to play. But many times the reverse occurs. A new puppy can spark new life into an older dog; the older dog will run around and play like he did years ago!

If cats are not in the mood to play with the puppy they will generally retreat and avoid the situation. But if your puppy persists he may get a "pop" on the nose from your cat. The puppy will quickly learn who enjoys his company and who doesn't!

Introducing adult dogs into an established household with other adult dogs and cats can sometimes be a problem. How well they get along really depends on the individual personalities of the animals involved. You can minimize stressful situations by close supervision of the initial interaction between your pets. If you sense any tension between your new Lhasa and the other animals, let them all have their own "space" and let them gradually get to know each other. Initially, don't force them to interact if they don't want to be together. Time will soften their stances. Be patient. Reassure

your pets that they are all loved and wanted. If you suspect any resentment or aggression, separate your new Lhasa from the other pets while you're away and can't supervise them. Also keep in mind that neutered pets tend to be less aggressive and territorial and will tolerate each other's company with less friction.

Collars and Leashes

Every dog needs a collar and a leash. These are the essential pieces of equipment for training and restraining your pet. The collar also serves another important function. Personalized identification tags and local rabies vaccination tags (if required) can be attached to the collar. These tags will avert much grief in the event your Lhasa is lost.

Most collars are made of nylon, leather, or steel. Make sure the collar fits properly. Check the collar frequently; as your puppy grows you will need to adjust it accordingly.

A training collar is essential for your puppy during training exercises. The best training collars are made of steel. Avoid a collar that is too large for your Lhasa even if it means purchasing another one later on. There should only be 2 to 3 inches (5–7.6 cm) of slack when the training collar is pulled tight, so that during training the correctional tug on the leash is felt immediately. Get your puppy used to wearing a collar at an early age. He will soon forget it is even on.

Buy a leash that is well constructed. The last thing you want is for the leash to break when you are walking your Lhasa along a busy street. Braided leather or nylon webbing leashes work well. A 6-foot (2 m) leash is a good length. You may also want an additional leash that is considerably longer (20 feet [6 m]) for some training exercises or for walking your dog in open spaces where minimal restraint is needed.

Your New Dog at Home

Toys

Dogs love to chew and play with toys. It is imperative to provide your Lhasa with safe toys and objects for chewing. Toys stimulate the Lhasa puppy, relieve boredom, and enhance development of healthy teeth and gums. Provide your puppy with a variety of toys to play with and he will be less likely to destroy your valuable property.

Select toys that are nontoxic and won't break into small fragments that can be swallowed whole. Rawhide chews and nylon bones are excellent choices for a Lhasa puppy. Select a size appropriate for your pet. Avoid plastic objects or items that contain metal. Bones are generally not a good idea either. Small bones may splinter in a Lhasa's mouth or digestive tract. Chewing on large bones can prematurely wear down the enamel of a dog's teeth. Balls and rings that are large enough so your Lhasa cannot swallow them make good toys.

It is also not a good idea to encourage your puppy to play with clothing or shoes. That will set up a confusing situation for him. All your clothing will then become fair game and invariably the puppy will decide your most expensive pair of shoes is his favorite item to chew on!

Sleeping Quarters

In my experience, most Lhasa apsos are house pets. They adapt well to indoor living due to their small size and modest exercise needs. That is not to say, however, that Lhasas can't be kept outdoors. Harsh climates and cold temperatures are no strangers to the Lhasa apso. Their long, thick coats are testimony to this fact. Remember, the breed originated in the rugged Himalayan mountain region of Tibet. If anything, Lhasas are more susceptible to problems such as heat stroke associated with high temperatures, especially if their coats are particularly long. If your Lhasa is kept outdoors it is essential to keep him well groomed and free of mats.

Crates

For indoor living your Lhasa needs his own space to call home. We have already discussed how important the den is to your puppy for comfort and security. If you choose to use a crate for your puppy's den you can convert it to permanent sleeping quarters for your mature Lhasa. Buy a crate or carrier large enough for an adult Lhasa and partition off a part of it when your dog is a puppy so it will retain the cozy den-like quality. When your Lhasa matures and is housebroken, you can then remove the top of the crate to allow him freedom to come and go as he pleases. The crate is also handy when transporting or traveling with your pet. No matter where you go, your Lhasa will feel right at home in his own familiar bed.

Dog beds also work fine once your Lhasa is trained to sleep on them. There are lots of styles available from catalogs or pet stores. Of course you can make your own if so inclined. It need not be fancy to suit your pet's needs. A wooden box with a blanket for bedding material is quite acceptable. No matter what style you choose, consider how easy it will be to clean and disinfect. Periodically it will need to be treated for fleas and ticks if they are a problem in your area. Wicker baskets look nice but are not always easy to clean. Some dogs will also chew on the wicker.

Let common sense dictate where the crate or bed should be placed. Avoid drafty areas and close proximity to heaters and air conditioners. Locate the bed where there is human contact, but not in the way of direct foot traffic, so your Lhasa can survey the action without being directly involved.

Doghouses

Whether building or buying a doghouse for your Lhasa, keep in mind its two main functions: to protect your dog from the elements, and to provide a place where your Lhasa can feel safe and secure.

17

Your New Dog at Home

It should be large enough for your dog to stretch out in all directions without touching the sides and tall enough for him to stand up without any difficulty. If the doghouse is too spacious your Lhasa won't feel as secure.

The traditional doghouse has been made out of wood with a shingle roof. Now doghouses can be purchased that are constructed of molded plastics, fiberglass, and other synthetic materials. They are durable and easy to clean. If you live in a cold climate you'll want to make sure the doghouse is insulated. To keep it dry and well ventilated, mount it 4 to 6 inches (10.1–15.2 cm) above the ground.

Traveling with Your Lhasa

Planning a vacation? Or moving across the country? There will probably come a time when you will consider taking your pet along with you when traveling. With careful planning and advance preparation, taking your Lhasa on a trip with you can be a lot of fun. After all, we do consider our pets members of the family, don't we? And there is no place your Lhasa would rather be than right alongside its owner and master, wherever that may be.

Of course where you are going and the length of your stay will also influence your decision as to whether it is appropriate to take your Lhasa with you on your trip. Traveling to a hotel in downtown Manhattan in New York City would probably be a miserable trip for you and your dog!

There are several possibilities concerning your Lhasa, however, that would *not* make it a good candidate for a traveling companion. It's best not to take a young puppy or a very old dog with you. If your Lhasa is sick or recovering from an illness leave him or her at home. Nervous, high-strung, or aggressive dogs will not make good travelers. Lastly, make sure your Lhasa does not suffer from motion sickness before embarking on your journey. Your veterinarian may be able to prescribe some antinausea medication if the need arises.

If, after careful consideration, you have decided not to take your Lhasa, you may board him at a kennel or veterinary hospital that provides boarding facilities. Or you can elect to have a responsible neighbor or friend care for your pet. It is less stressful on your pet if the same feeding and exercise routine is maintained in your absence. Be sure you leave your veterinarian's phone number and a number where you can be reached in case of an emergency.

If you have decided your vacation would not be complete without your canine pal, by all means take him along! Before you leave, however, plan ahead. This will save you lots of headaches and inconveniences once you are underway. First, take your pet to your veterinarian to make sure he or she is healthy to travel. Immunizations for rabies, distemper, parvovirus, etc., should be current. Heartworm and fecal checks for parasites are also a good idea. Obtain a vaccine certificate or a copy of your pet's medical records. This is especially valuable if your Lhasa has any chronic medical problems. If your Lhasa is on medication, be sure you have plenty to last the entire trip because it may be difficult getting a prescription refilled away from home.

Traveling By Air

When traveling by air, check with your airline for specific recommendations concerning your pet. Most carriers require a health certificate signed by a veterinarian certifying your pet is currently vaccinated against rabies and is free of any signs of communicable disease. In the United States, the health certificate must be dated within 10 days of departure. If you don't already own a traveling crate, one can be rented or purchased from the airline company. Feed and water your Lhasa lightly two to three hours before boarding the plane. Tranquilizers for your pet during the flight are generally not needed. Your veterinarian can counsel you best on your specific needs in this matter.

If you're planning a trip to a foreign country with

Your New Dog at Home

When traveling with your Lhasa, a carrier provides security and comfort in unfamiliar surroundings.

your Lhasa, find out the requirements for entry well in advance of departure. Contact the country's consulate for the most accurate and up-to-date information.

Some countries require a pet to be quarantined prior to entry. England, Australia, and Hawaii, for example, impose four to six months' quarantine of dogs prior to entry.

Traveling By Car

Get your Lhasa accustomed to riding in the car by gradually starting with short trips around town. When your Lhasa perceives the car as an extension of his household, he'll feel at home on the road. Therefore bring along familiar items, such as bowls and bedding material. A crate is also highly recommended. Having his own crate will make your pet feel comfortable and secure and help prevent him from distracting the driver and possibly causing an accident. Many hotels and motels allow well-behaved pets in their rooms. To find suitable accomodations check travel guides and auto clubs. It is always a good idea to call and confirm your lodgings ahead of time. A word of caution about cars and pets. Never leave your Lhasa unattended in a parked car when it's over 60°F (16°C) and sunny outside. The temperature inside a parked car with the windows only partially rolled up can reach 120°F (48.9°C). Your Lhasa can quickly become overheated and develop heat stroke, which is a life-threatening condition requiring immediate medical attention. One final word about traveling with your pet. Remember, you are responsible for your dog's behavior. Be considerate of your fellow travelers in this regard. Enjoy your trip!

The Proper Diet

Since people have become more health conscious, dog owners also want to make sure their canine friends get the most out of life by eating a complete and well-balanced diet.

Over the years we have become much more knowledgeable and sophisticated about dogs' nutritional needs. For example, we can treat bladder stones and kidney disease with special prescription diet foods. It is now known that a Lhasa's nutritional needs change as he or she grows older.

Every dog needs a balanced diet for optimum growth and development. A poor diet can lead to a variety of medical, developmental, and behavioral problems. Even if only one essential nutrient is missing or not in the correct proportion your Lhasa will suffer. That is why I do not recommend trying to prepare a homemade diet for your Lhasa. In a homemade diet it is difficult to balance the correct proportions of the essential nutrients, which are proteins, carbohydrates, fats, vitamins, and minerals. If you must prepare a homemade ration please consult a veterinarian for the correct formulation.

The rules for establishing a sound nutritional program for your Lhasa are really quite simple. First, use a good, high-quality dog food that agrees with your pet and second, do not overfeed him. As a veterinarian I spend a considerable part of my day counseling clients on these two points. Everyone loves to see their pet eat—just don't overdo it; we can love them to death!

Basic Nutrition

The basic elements of a balanced diet for your Lhasa are proteins, carbohydrates, fats, vitamins, minerals, and water. Let's discuss each individual component so you can better understand a Lhasa's nutritional needs.

Protein sources in your dog's diet include meat and poultry products, fish, eggs, soybeans, and corn. After protein is ingested it is broken down in the small intestines into primary components called amino acids. These amino acids in turn are recombined in the liver and other tissues to form new protein specific for your dog. These proteins are necessary for many functions, such as growth and repair of muscle and bone, antibodies to fight infections, and making new red blood cells to carry oxygen.

Because puppies are growing rapidly, pound for pound they require higher levels of protein than mature dogs. In fact, many old dogs are put on restricted protein diets because excess protein in the diet must be metabolized and eliminated and this just adds more burden to the geriatric liver and kidneys.

Carbohydrates supply energy for the Lhasa. Carbohydrates are measured in calories. These calories provide the "fuel" to drive your pet's metabolic engine. Common sources of carbohydrates are grains, starches, and vegetables.

Fats and Oils are a concentrated source of energy. There is twice as much energy in a gram of fat than a gram of carbohydrate or protein. Fat is also necessary for your Lhasa to utilize the fat-soluble vitamins A, D, E, and K. Maintaining healthy skin, coat, and nervous system depends on dietary fat.

Vitamins function as the catalysts to drive chemical reactions in the body. Some vitamins are not required in the diet. For instance, dogs can synthesize their own vitamin C (humans cannot). However, most vitamins must come from the food your Lhasa consumes.

Minerals are necessary for the Lhasa's health. Tooth, bone, and muscle development depend on calcium and phosphorous. Sodium, chloride, and potassium are necessary to maintain body fluids and a healthy nervous system. Iron is a vital component of hemoglobin, which is found in red blood cells and carries oxygen throughout the body. Other trace elements such as copper, manganese, selenium, and zinc are also essential but are needed in very small quantities.

The ratios of vitamins and minerals to each

The Proper Diet

other is extremely important. Usually the problem is oversupplementation resulting in potentially toxic levels of these substances. Vitamin and mineral supplements should only be given after consulting with your veterinarian.

Water is the most abundant substance found in a dog, accounting for approximately 70 percent of a dog's total weight. Don't take it for granted—provide plenty of fresh, clean water at all times.

Commercial Dog Food

Fortunately, high-quality commercial dog foods that are palatable, nutritious, and convenient to use are now available for all dog owners. When considering types of dog food to feed your Lhasa, the adage "you get what you pay for" rings loud and clear. For your Lhasa's optimum health and thick, rich coat stick to the high-quality brands. They cost

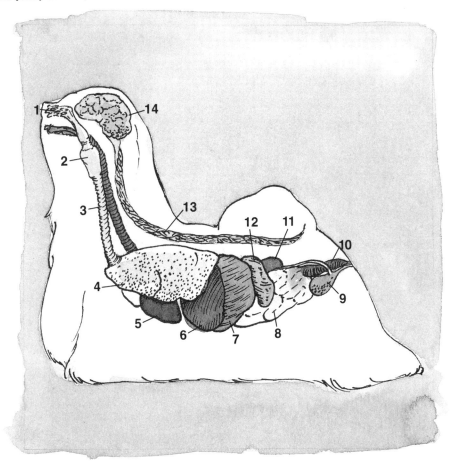

The major internal organs of the Lhasa Apso.
1. nasal sinus 2. larynx 3. trachea 4. lungs 5. heart 6. liver 7. stomach 8. intestine 9. bladder 10. rectum 11. kidneys 12. spleen 13. spinal cord

more per pound but their nutrient quality is superior, making them more digestible. Besides, due to a Lhasa's relatively small size and appetite, the slight increase in cost is not that significant.

Whatever dog food you choose, be sure it is labeled "nutritionally complete and balanced." Dog-food brands that carry this label have met or exceeded the standards for good nutrition set by the National Research Council. Beware of all meat diets. They are nutritionally incomplete. Avoid generic dog foods. These generally contain low-quality nutrients that are poorly digested, resulting in poor hair coat and bulky stools, and are not thrifty. Premium dog foods contain nutrients of high digestability that are easily absorbed and do not pass through the digestive tract as unusable waste. Hence there is also less stool to clean up.

Commercial dog foods are available in three general types—dry, semimoist, and canned.

Dry Dog Food contains about 10 percent moisture. Since most of the water is removed, dry food is the most concentrated in terms of energy, providing approximately 100 calories per ounce. Plenty of water should always be made available. Dogs have less tendency to overeat dry food. Because it is hard and crunchy, dry food contributes to maintaining healthy teeth and gums.

Semimoist Food is about 20 to 35 percent moisture and contains about 75 to 85 calories per ounce. It is very convenient and generally quite palatable because of its meatlike texture and consistency.

Canned Food contains approximately 75 percent moisture and provides 30 to 40 calories per ounce. Because of its high water content, canned food will spoil if left out at room temperature. Any unused portion should be refrigerated. Canned food tends to be highly palatable—but be careful; some canned foods contain high levels of sodium and fat. Dogs love the taste but may overeat, leading to obesity and other medical problems associated with high-fat diets.

Once you have chosen a particular brand of dog food to feed your Lhasa the next question is, How much do I feed my dog? The answer depends on such factors as your Lhasa's age, size, activity level, and individual metabolism. The feeding recommendations on dog-food labels are only guidelines. You must tailor the amount to feed to your own Lhasa. It's best to judge by your Lhasa's weight and appearance—it should have a tapering waist and the ribs should be easily felt. If you're not sure, your veterinarian can advise you as to your dog's ideal weight. You can then adjust the amount of food accordingly.

Vitamin and Mineral Supplements should be used cautiously. They are needed in very small quantities and some vitamins and minerals can be toxic if given to excess. Did you know that a popular rat poison in the United States works by overdosing rats with vitamin D? There are circumstances when your Lhasa may need vitamins and minerals. For example, if your Lhasa is anemic (not enough red blood cells), iron and B vitamins are helpful to regenerate new red blood cells. Your veterinarian can advise you specifically about any supplements your Lhasa may need. As a general rule, if your Lhasa is on a high-quality dog food diet and has no active health problems, vitamin and mineral supplements are unnecessary. The proper amounts and proportions of vitamins and minerals are already included in the dog food.

Everyone likes to give their dog treats or biscuits. There is no harm in this so long as it's not overdone. They should be given as a reward for good behavior, not as a staple of your Lhasa's diet. Some commercially prepared dog biscuits provide complete and balanced nutrition. Check the label. With these biscuits you will be assured that your Lhasa is maintaining a balanced diet.

I would discourage giving your Lhasa table food and scraps on a regular basis. Feeding your Lhasa table scraps, especially at the dinner table, will encourage begging. If your dog doesn't expect anything from the dinner table he won't beg. Begging can be a difficult habit to break. So it is wise not to let it get started. Also, your Lhasa may decide not to eat his regular dog food if he knows he will get table scraps later on. This may cause an im-

The Proper Diet

Lhasas, like most dogs, love to eat. By feeding a high quality dog food, you don't have to sacrifice flavor and palatability for good nutrition.

balance in your pet's diet. Furthermore, one of the biggest problems I see every day in my practice associated with feeding table scraps is that of dogs becoming overweight. People think a little treat here and there will not make any difference, but if you weigh only five pounds it can make a big difference. For example, if a 15-pound Lhasa received a 1½-ounce piece of meat, proportionately, a person weighing 160 pounds would have to eat an entire pound. Some treat!

Feeding Puppies (Eight Weeks to One Year)

The key to your puppy's health and proper development is a complete and well-balanced diet designed for puppies. On a pound for pound basis, puppies require twice as many calories and nutrients as an adult dog. Good-quality puppy foods contain the extra nutrients your puppy needs. Don't

skimp on puppy food. Do your Lhasa a favor by providing high-quality feed and establishing correct eating habits.

A two- to six-month-old puppy should be fed three to four times daily. Feed a six- to twelve-month-old puppy twice daily. Generally, it is best to feed your Lhasa puppy all it can eat in about five minutes. Avoid in-between meal snacks. This encourages bad habits at an early age that can be difficult to break later. If you want to give your puppy milk give small amounts gradually because milk may give your puppy diarrhea.

Feeding Young Dogs (One to Seven Years)

Your Lhasa puppy will physically mature at approximately 10 to 12 months of age. His bones will stop growing and his nutritional needs will change. His weight should begin to stabilize. At this age, your Lhasa can begin eating an adult dog food. One to two feedings per day is sufficient for your adult Lhasa. As I have stressed before, the amount to feed needs to be tailored to each individual dog. Some Lhasas will manage their own weight very well if they are allowed free access to dry food. I have found most Lhasas will not overeat dry dog food under these circumstances. Table scraps and between-meal snacks are usually the culprits that are responsible for overweight Lhasas (See section on Obesity, page 41).

Feeding Older Dogs (Eight Years and Older)

As your Lhasa grows older, he will become less active and his metabolism will slow down. His energy (calory) and protein needs will decrease ac-

The Proper Diet

cordingly. Therefore a ten-year old Lhasa should not be fed as much as when he was three or four years old. There are now some excellent commercial dog foods available that are made specifically for older dogs. These dog foods are lower in calories yet still contain all the necessary nutrients, vitamins, and minerals for a complete and balanced diet. If your Lhasa develops medical problems as he ages, such as diabetes, colitis, heart or kidney disease, your veterinarian may precribe specific diets to help combat these ailments. For example, dog foods low in salt are used to treat heart conditions and dogs with kidney diseases benefit from restricted protein diets.

Grooming

If you want your Lhasa to look and feel its very best, a regular grooming program is essential. All Lhasas need to be combed, brushed, and bathed routinely to keep their coats healthy, shiny, and free of mats. Care of the toenails, eyes, ears, and teeth are also important to keep your Lhasa looking good and staying healthy. Keep in mind grooming is not just for cosmetic purposes. A Lhasa's long, thick coat acts as insulation to protect it from heat or cold. If your Lhasa's coat becomes matted this insulating quality will be lost. Severely matted hair cannot be untangled and will have to be cut out. Mats are also good hiding places for fleas and ticks. By regularly brushing and bathing your Lhasa you'll be doing him another favor. In the grooming process, you are constantly evaluating his overall appearance, checking his skin, eyes, ears, etc., for anything unusual. Red eyes, foul-smelling ears, lumps, or sore spots of skin may need medical attention and are easier to treat if detected early.

Many Lhasa owners delegate most of the grooming to a professional. I would highly recommend utilizing a professional groomer if you are not inclined to spend the considerable time and effort to learn the proper grooming techniques. Most groomers charge a reasonable fee for their services. They will be able to advise you as to how you want your Lhasa clipped and combed. Your other choice, of course, is to do the grooming yourself. Here are some tips that will help make grooming an enjoyable experience for you and your pet. First, start grooming your Lhasa when he or she is still a puppy. Puppies will accept bathing, brushing, and nail trimming easier than a mature dog. Puppies' attention spans are short, so start with brushing sessions that last no longer than five minutes. Expose your puppy to the sound of clippers and running water before grooming so he won't be afraid of them when you are ready to begin. Above all, make grooming a positive experience for your Lhasa. Talk to him in a smooth, comforting voice. Give him lots of encouragement and praise him when you are finished. Reward good behavior with a treat or take him for a walk. Your Lhasa will associate grooming with a pleasant experience and will be eager for his next session.

Brushing and Combing

Brushing and combing your Lhasa removes dead hair, distributes oil in the fur, and helps prevent formation of mats. To begin, select a comfortable place to work. A table top or bench is a good choice, or even your lap if you want and if your Lhasa is steady and will remain calm.

It is important to comb all the way down to the roots next to the skin, beginning at the end of the hair. If you find a mat, try to untangle it with your fingers before combing through it. Then tease the hair free with the comb starting at the outside edge of the mat. Knots that you can't untangle will have to be cut out with a blunt pair of scissors. Be careful not to cut the skin. Consult your groomer or veterinarian if you dog is severely matted.

The long hair on the crown of the Lhasa's head may be controlled by plaiting, barrettes, or clipping.

Grooming

Frequent brushing is necessary to keep the Lhasa Apso's long coat in optimal condition.

Bathing

Bathe your Lhasa no more than is necessary. Too much bathing will dry out a Lhasa's skin and remove natural oils from its coat. If your Lhasa loves to roll in the mud (or worse) or has flea problems, more frequent shampooing is called for. Always remove mats before bathing because they will be even harder to untangle when they are wet.

Choose a shampoo made especially for dogs. Harsh detergents will damage your Lhasa's coat and skin. Shampoos are available to kill fleas and ticks. Check with your veterinarian if your pet has any skin problems. He or she may prescribe a medicated shampoo for your dog.

For bathing indoors, the bathtub or, for puppies, the sink are good locations. Use common sense when bathing your Lhasa outdoors. Your pet can get chilled if it's too cold or windy because its fur loses the ability to insulate when it's wet. To protect your dog's eyes, apply a drop or two of mineral oil or eye salve to them before you begin bathing. Next, wet the coat thoroughly with warm water. A hand-held shower attachment is very convenient. Massage the shampoo through the hair, working your way to the skin. Most dogs like the attention and will appreciate the rubdown they receive. Be thorough but avoid getting shampoo in the eyes and ears. Flea and medicated shampoos should be worked in well and allowed to remain on the coat for at least 10 minutes to assure proper action. Shampoos should be rinsed off your pet thoroughly with warm water. Some medicated dips are designed to remain on your pet and should not be rinsed off. Unless you're quick with a towel, be prepared to get wet at this point, because your Lhasa will love to shake the water out of his fur. A hand-held blow dryer is handy to speed up the drying process. Always comb your Lhasa while he or she is still wet to prevent matting. Avoid brushing because it can damage wet hair.

Care of the Toenails

Lhasas need to have their toenails clipped occasionally, especially if they spend most of their time indoors and thus don't wear their nails down on hard surfaces. Overgrown nails, if unchecked, can actually grow into the foot pads causing pain and infections.

Since most dogs are not eager to have their nails trimmed (or feet worked on in general), get them

Lhasas' individual personalities will begin to emerge when they reach about five weeks of age. They may all seem equally irresistible, but by observing carefully, you will soon see that they vary in assertiveness, independence, and curiosity.

Grooming

To determine how much nail to trim, imagine a straight line from the bottom of the pad to the toenail. This will help you avoid cutting the quick. The guillotine-type nail trimmer shown here, works well.

accustomed to it at an early age. Your Lhasa will grow up accepting nail clipping as part of its normal routine.

Toenail trimming is not a difficult procedure, but care must be taken not to clip too much. Hold your Lhasa's paw securely so it won't pull away as you trim the nail. Avoid cutting into the quick (nerve and blood vessel in the nail) because this will

Above: Lhasas generally make excellent mothers. In most cases they will tend their puppies carefully, keeping them clean and well fed. Below: A mother nursing her puppies.

cause the toenail to bleed and is also painful to your Lhasa. Digital pressure with a styptic pencil will stop the bleeding, but I guarantee you that trimming your Lhasa's toenails will become quite a battle if previous nail-trimming episodes resulted in painful cries and bleeding nails. I have had clients tell me their dogs have become so afraid of toenail clipping that they hide whenever they see their owner bring out the nail clippers! If you have any doubts about your nail-trimming ability, let your veterinarian or groomer trim the nails for you or show you how it's done properly.

I also advise trimming the hair between the foot pads on the underside of the paws. This will help prevent knotting of the hair which is uncomfortable to your pet and can cause irritation and sores between the pads. It's also a good idea to trim the hair around the anus to prevent fecal matter from soiling the area.

Care of the Eyes and Ears

Care of the eyes and ears should also be part of any grooming routine. Check for any mucus accumulating around the eyes and gently remove it with a tissue. With a pair of blunt scissors, you may want to trim some of the hair around the eyes to prevent irritation and excessive tearing. Consult your veterinarian if you notice any ocular discharge, redness of the eyes, or excessive squinting.

The ears need to be examined on a regular basis. If the hair growth inside the ear canal becomes thickened or matted with wax it will need to be plucked out. The hair can be removed with a pair of tweezers or forceps. Surprisingly enough, most dogs do not object to having hair pulled out of the ear canal. Wax and debris can be removed from the ear canal with a cleaning solution obtained from your veterinarian. If the ears are red, overly sensitive, or foul smelling, seek medical attention promptly.

Grooming

Care of the Teeth

We all know how important it is to take care of our own teeth. Your Lhasa's dental health is equally important to his overall well-being. Care of the teeth and gums should begin when your Lhasa is still a puppy.

Puppies, like babies, are born without teeth. When puppies reach four to eight weeks of age their deciduous or baby teeth will emerge. These temporary teeth, 28 altogether, are small and sharp. Puppies will begin losing deciduous teeth when they are about four months old. This is when they will begin teething and they will want to chew on everything they can find. Provide them with plenty of chew toys such as nylon bones and rawhide sticks. If you don't, your Lhasa puppy may find its own chew toys, like your favorite pair of shoes! When

Check your Lhasa's front and rear teeth regularly for tartar and plaque build-up.

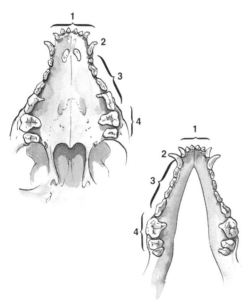

The Lhasa Apso's permanent teeth.
Upper teeth: 1. incisors (six) 2. canines (two) 3. premolars (eight) 4. molars (four). Lower teeth: 1. incisors (six) 2. canines (two) 3. premolars (eight) 4. molars (six).

your Lhasa is between six to eight months old all the deciduous teeth should be gone and replaced by permanent adult teeth. The incisors at the front of the mouth are the first adult teeth to erupt, followed by the canines (fang). The premolars and molars are the last permanent teeth to emerge. Sometimes the deciduous teeth do not fall out as they should. If these retained deciduous teeth remain in the mouth too long they can cause the permanent teeth to be misaligned. The retained deciduous teeth should be extracted. Check with your veterinarian if you suspect any problems.

The next challenge is to keep all of your Lhasa's 42 adult teeth clean and healthy. Feeding dry food and biscuits will help clean the teeth and promote healthy gums. But don't expect a good diet alone to prevent all dental problems. The most common dental problem in dogs is periodontal (gum) disease. Dental experts claim that more than 90 percent of dogs over three years old have some degree of periodontal disease. This condition begins when bacteria, saliva, and decaying food combine to form a sticky film on the teeth called plaque. As the plaque builds up, a cementlike substance called tartar develops, usually starting at the gum line. It is yellow to brown in color and can eventually spread to cover the entire tooth. As the gums are inflamed by the tartar, bacteria infect the root of the tooth and cause erosion of the surrounding bone that secures the tooth. Eventually, the root is destroyed and the tooth will fall out. Signs of periodontal disease are red, inflamed gums, presence of tartar, and bad breath. If your Lhasa is showing any of these signs, take him to your veterinarian. Your pet's teeth may need a professional cleaning. If any teeth are very loose or decayed they should be extracted to prevent further problems. Your veterinarian can also demonstrate how to brush your dog's teeth. Brushing is one of the best ways to prevent tartar build-up. If you start brushing when your Lhasa is young, he or she will be more likely to accept it. Use a soft child's toothbrush or gauze pad and baking soda or canine toothpaste. Human toothpaste may foam excessively and tends to upset your dog's stomach.

Medical Care for Your Lhasa

You and the Veterinarian

Your Lhasa depends on you for practically everything. With pet ownership also comes a responsibility to keep the pet healthy and provide the best care you possibly can.

Nobody is more knowledgeable or better trained to keep your Lhasa healthy than a veterinarian. Veterinarians all share similar educational backgrounds. To earn their veterinary degree, they spend four years in veterinary school following four years of preveterinary science education. Upon graduation they must pass state and national board certification tests to obtain a license to practice.

It is important to develop a good rapport with your veterinarian, because you will be relying on him or her for advice and expertise on a wide range of topics throughout your dog's life. If you don't have a veterinarian yet ask your friends and neighbors who they recommend.

Don't be afraid to ask your veterinarian questions. Communication is the key to a good client-doctor relationship. Make sure everything is explained to you in terminology you can understand. Remember, the more you know about your dog, the better you will be able to accurately answer questions your vet may ask you concerning your pet. Accurate information concerning your dog's behavior is important in making a diagnosis.

If your Lhasa ever does get sick, be sure to follow your veterinarian's instructions exactly.

Preventive Care for Your Lhasa

The best way to keep your Lhasa healthy is to prevent problems before they start. You can accomplish that by providing proper care at home and taking your pet to your veterinarian for vaccination and routine checkups.

Immunizations (vaccines) protect your pet from certain infections by stimulating his or her immune system to produce disease-fighting antibodies.

Examination of a Lhasa's eyes by a veterinarian is part of a routine physical exam.

Initially a puppy receives antibodies from his mother's milk. After a few weeks the antibodies are no longer effective, leaving your puppy unprotected and vulnerable to disease. This is why puppies should be vaccinated at an early age.

Puppies should be immunized when they reach six to eight weeks of age. Your puppy should receive a series of shots at three- to four-week intervals until he or she is fourteen to sixteen weeks old and will then be checked for parasites, both internal and external, and treated if necessary (see vaccination schedule, page 34).

Adult dogs should be revaccinated annually to maintain immunity. During the annual visit your veterinarian will examine your pet and discuss any health problems with you. Laboratory tests to check for parasites may be necessary.

The following are descriptions of the infections that can be prevented by vaccination. Your veterinarian can recommend a specific vaccination program for your pet.

Medical Care for Your Lhasa

Diseases Preventable by Immunization

Distemper

Canine distemper is a highly contagious viral disease that occurs world wide and affects dogs and other animals such as foxes, wolves, ferrets, skunks, and raccoons. In the past, canine distemper killed more puppies than any other disease. Fortunately, due to the widespread use of an effective vaccine, its incidence has been reduced and this fatal disease can be prevented in dogs.

Typically, most canine distemper infections occur in unvaccinated puppies and young adults. Infection occurs from exposure to an infected animal or contaminated object. Symptoms of distemper usually appear six to nine days after exposure to the virus. Initially, signs of a cold develop, such as fever and mucus discharge from the nose and eyes. At this point, most infected dogs are listless, have a poor appetite, and sometimes develop diarrhea. In some cases, the skin on the foot pads and nose becomes thickened. This is known as "hard pad" disease. Some dogs may seem to recover from the initial symptoms described above, and then later develop nervous signs such as muscle twitching in the face and legs, incoordination, paralysis, or convulsive seizures.

Since there is no specific cure for distemper, treatment is often unrewarding. Vaccination is the key to preventing this disease.

Rabies

Rabies is a potentially fatal disease caused by a virus. All warm-blooded animals (including man) are susceptible. It occurs most commonly in dogs, cats, and wild carnivores such as foxes, skunks, raccoons, and bats. Rabies occurs worldwide except in some areas where it has been eradicated, such as England and Hawaii. Strict quarantine regulations are enforced in rabies-free countries to prevent its introduction.

Rabies is usually transmitted through the bite of an infected animal carrying the virus in its saliva. The incubation period (which is how long it takes symptoms to appear after exposure to the virus) is usually between 10 to 50 days and occasionally longer—up to several months—depending on the location of the bite and how long it takes the virus to reach the brain.

Rabies is a disease of the central nervous system. There are classically two forms of the disease. The paralytic form ("dumb" rabies), is characterized by paralysis of the muscles of the jaw and throat. Inability to swallow, profuse salivation, and drooping of the lower jaw are signs seen in dogs. In the furious form ("mad dog" syndrome), dogs may become aggressive and irritable. They may lose all caution and fear of natural enemies, and any noise may initiate attack.

There is no effective treatment for rabies after the onset of clinical signs in dogs or man. Any suspected rabid animal should not be approached. The police and animal-control officers should be alerted.

If you are bitten by any suspected rabid animal immediately scrub the wound with soap and water and get prompt medical attention.

Control of rabies is by immunization. Most states and local municipalities require rabies vaccines for dogs. Check with your local veterinarian for your Lhasa's rabies vaccine requirements and licensing.

Parvovirus

This is a viral disease that affects the intestinal tract of dogs. Any unvaccinated dog is susceptible, although young puppies from 6 to 16 weeks of age are most seriously affected. The first signs of parvovirus infection are listlessness and loss of appetite. Soon vomiting and profuse, watery, and sometimes bloody diarrhea develop. These symptoms in puppies can be very acute and cause severe dehydration. Death may soon follow if the disease is untreated. Many times prompt veterinary atten-

Medical Care for Your Lhasa

tion can save your puppy's life. Your vet will administer fluids to correct dehydration and antibiotics to prevent secondary infection.

Parvovirus is highly contagious to unvaccinated dogs, and many times an entire litter will become infected.

In very young puppies, usually under eight weeks of age, parvovirus can infect the heart muscle and cause sudden death due to heart failure.

Leptospirosis

This is a bacterial disease affecting dogs that can also infect man. The most common modes of transmission are water contaminated with urine from an infected animal or by direct contact with an infected animal.

Symptoms of leptospirosis include fever, loss of appetite, vomiting, diarrhea, and, as the disease progresses, dogs may become jaundiced, have a painful abdomen, weak rear legs, and exhibit ulcers in the mouth. Serious kidney and liver damage can result from exposure to this disease.

Hepatitis

Infectious canine hepatitis can range from a mild illness to a fatal infection. This viral disease can affect dogs of all ages.

An infected dog will run a fever, show inappetence and lethargy, and may have a very painful abdomen. Other symptoms include tonsillitis, vomiting, and hemorrhaging from the oral mucus membranes. Some dogs deteriorate very rapidly and die within 24 hours after clinical signs appear. Infected dogs need intensive care by a veterinarian. Some dogs that recover develop a cloudy corneal opacity (hepatitis blue eye) which usually disappears spontaneously.

Parainfluenza

This virus is one of the causes of tracheobronchitis, which has inadvertently been labeled "kennel cough"! This is unfortunate, because dogs don't have to be in a kennel to contract this infection. Since this disease is highly contagious, especially where dogs are in close proximity to one another,

Vaccination Schedule

DISEASE	AGE AT 1ST VACCINE (WEEKS)	AGE AT 2ND VACCINE (WEEKS)	AGE AT 3RD VACCINE (WEEKS)	REVACCINATION
DHLP-P (Distemper, hepatitis, leptospirosis, parainfluenza, parvovirus)	6–8	10–12	14–16	Annually
Corona	6–8	10–12	14–16	Annually
Bordetella	Give at least 1 week prior to group confinement.			Annually
Rabies	12–16			Every 1–3 years depending on local and state laws and the type of vaccine administered

34

Medical Care for Your Lhasa

many kennels require all dogs be immunized before admittance to the boarding facility.

The classic sign of tracheobronchitis is a dry, hacking cough followed by wretching or gagging which are attempts to clear the throat of any mucus. The coughing spells tend to occur in cycles and are activated by excitement or activity. Mild pressure applied to the trachea (windpipe) will induce coughing. Most dogs have a normal appetite and remain fairly active and alert unless the coughing is severe and continuous. If untreated, secondary infections can develop, producing serious respiratory problems; relapses are common. Tracheobronchitis can be treated by your veterinarian. Dogs with this malady should be isolated from other dogs because of its highly contagious nature.

Corona and Bordetella

There are two new vaccines that are now available to protect your Lhasa apso against corona virus and bordetella bacterial infections. These diseases are highly contagious and spread very quickly through dogs in close contact with each other. For this reason these vaccines are especially recommended for dogs on the show circuit and pets that will be boarding or traveling frequently.

Corona Virus infection typically causes a watery, foul-smelling, sometimes bloody diarrhea. If untreated, dogs may become severely dehydrated and fatalities can occur. Dogs of all ages are susceptible. Corona virus infections can be difficult to distinguish from parvovirus.

Bordetella is a bacteria that is associated with the tracheobronchitis disease complex. Vaccinating against bordetella provides an extra measure of protection for your Lhasa.

Keeping Your Lhasa Parasite Free

Parasites pose a lifelong threat to the health of your Lhasa apso. Parasites are not only debilitating themselves, they may transmit other diseases, and some parasites are a public-health concern. Since puppies are the most susceptible to parasites they should be checked at an early age. Whenever the presence of parasites is detected, the animal should be treated promptly by your veterinarian.

Internal Parasites

Your Lhasa apso should be checked for internal parasites by your veterinarian as part of a routine health examination whether it is your first puppy visit or an annual checkup. These parasites are usually best diagnosed by a microscopic examination of a fresh stool specimen. General symptoms of internal parasites may include lethargy, weight loss, diarrhea, or bloated abdomen.

Unfortunately, no one drug is effective in eliminating all the different types of internal parasites your dog may have. For this reason, many over-the-counter wormers are ineffective. It is best to leave detection, diagnosis, and treatment of internal parasites to your veterinarian. He or she can administer the safest and most effective medication for your dog's particular parasites.

To help prevent internal parasitic reinfection, remove fecal material from your yard regularly and dispose of it in a sanitary manner.

Roundworms

The most common type of roundworm found in dogs is called *Toxocara canis*. Adult worms are about 5 inches (12.7 cm) long and may be passed in the stools or vomitus.

Although a dog of any age is susceptible, puppies are at the highest risk and are usually infected in the womb prior to birth.

Adult roundworms live in the small intestines. Larval forms may migrate to the lungs and other parts of the body. Eggs are found in the feces and can only be seen under a microscope.

Puppies with roundworms may exhibit poor

growth; they are often lackluster and typically have a "potbellied" appearance. Other symptoms sometimes observed are vomiting, diarrhea, and respiratory difficulties due to larval migration through the lungs.

If roundworms are found by your veterinarian, your Lhasa puppy will be treated at that time. Your vet will probably want to recheck a stool sample at a later date to make sure all the adults and larvae have been killed and re-treat if necessary. Prompt disposal of fecal material and good sanitation at home will help prevent reinfection.

Hookworms

These are small blood-sucking worms that attach to the small intestine. They are rarely seen in the feces and are diagnosed by eggs found in a microscopic examination of the stool.

Adult dogs are infected by either direct ingestion of larvae or larval penetration of the skin. Puppies are usually infected by larval transmission through the mother's placenta or breast milk.

Symptoms of hookworm infection are poor appetite, weight loss, listlessness, tarry or bloody stools, and pale gums. Since hookworms suck blood, they can rapidly cause a fatal anemia, especially in puppies. Consult your veterinarian immediately if any of these signs are present.

To prevent reinfection do not allow your dog in contaminated areas and dispose of all feces promptly.

Tapeworms

Tapeworms are flat, segmented worms that live in the intestines and may reach several feet in length. They feed on intestinal contents.

The most common types of tapeworms are transmitted by fleas and rodents. Therefore, flea control will eliminate many reinfections.

Tapeworms rarely cause serious disease in dogs. Signs, if present, may vary from unthriftiness with food (despite a good appetite) to irritability and diarrhea. Sometimes dogs will try to relieve their

The canine tapeworm cannot complete it's life cycle without developing in it's intermediate host, the flea. When an infected flea is ingested by a dog, the tapeworm matures in the animal's small intestine. Tapeworm eggs may also be found in raw meat or fish.

anus itch because of irritation by the tapeworm segments by scooting around on their rump.

Tapeworms are diagnosed by finding tapeworm segments that resemble grains of rice in the stool. Dried segments may be found around the anus or in the dog's bedding. Talk to your veterinarian for treatment to eliminate the tapeworm and to prevent reinfection.

Coccidia and Giardia

Coccidia and Giardia are microscopic, single-celled (protozoa) organisms that live in the small intestines. Although rarely a problem in older dogs, these parasites can be devastating to puppies. Diarrhea, which is sometimes profuse and watery, is the most common symptom, and may be accompanied by straining and gas. Chronic, low-grade infections result in weight loss despite a good appetite.

Diagnosis requires a microscopic examination of a *fresh* stool specimen.

Medical Care for Your Lhasa

Heartworms

This parasite is prevelant in certain geographic locations in the United States and elsewhere in the world. Your veterinarian can advise you as to the importance of this parasite in your area.

Heartworms are long, thin worms that live in the heart and blood vessels leading from the heart. This parasite is potentially very dangerous to your pet as it can cause serious, prolonged illness and death.

Heartworms are transmitted to dogs by mosquito bites. When a mosquito carrying heartworm larvae bites a dog, tiny larvae are released into the dog's bloodstream. After a series of molts these larvae develop into adult heartworms and migrate to the heart where they remain as adults. Approximately six months after infection the adult heartworms then produce offspring called microfilaria, and discharge them into the bloodstream where they are sucked up by mosquitoes that have bitten the infected dog. The cycle is completed when the infected mosquito bites an unprotected dog.

Symptoms of heartworm disease are coughing, weight loss, decreased exercise tolerance, and shortness of breath. In advanced cases, difficult breathing, abdominal distention, and collapse may also be seen.

Your veterinarian can test your dog's blood to detect heartworm disease. Treatment for heartworm disease is usually successful if diagnosed in the early stages. However, a powerful drug is required to kill the adult worms, and it is not without potential hazards.

Fortunately, heartworm disease can be easily prevented with safe, effective, and inexpensive medication that is given during mosquito season in your area (early spring to late fall in northern areas; all year round in some warm climates). Daily medication may be prescribed or a monthly medication is now available. Your veterinarian will want to test your dog's blood for the presence of heartworms before prescribing a preventive, because a dog that already is infected with heartworms may have a reaction to the preventive.

External Parasites

Fleas

Fleas are the most common external parasite found in dogs. Adult fleas are small, wingless parasites that will cause your dog to scratch. Because adult fleas feed on your dog's blood, heavy flea infestation of your dog can cause a serious anemia. Puppies are especially susceptible. Signs of anemia are lethargy, poor appetite, weight loss, and pale gums. Some dogs develop skin rashes, hair loss, and may itch intensely due to an allergy to flea bites. Tapeworms can be transmitted by fleas if your Lhasa ingests a flea while he is licking or grooming himself.

To control fleas, it is important to understand their life cycle. Fleas spend most of their life *off* the dog. Adult fleas spend time on your dog only to feed. Breeding, egg laying, and larval develop-

The life cycle of the canine heartworm. A mosquito bites a dog infected with heartworm. Larvae molt inside the mosquito, which injects infective larvae into another dog. Larvae develop into long, thread-like worms that reside in the heart, causing extensive damage to the heart and circulatory system.

Medical Care for Your Lhasa

ment of the flea take place in the environment—i.e., carpet and bedding for inside dogs, and yard, doghouse, etc., for outside dogs. Under optimum conditions (warmth and humidity) fleas can complete an entire life cycle in three weeks. Larval stages of the flea feed on organic matter in the environment and can remain viable for months if necessary. Fleas thrive from early summer to late fall in northern climates and are a problem all year long in warm, humid southern climates.

When trying to rid your dog of fleas it is important to treat both your pet and the environment. Flea foggers and premise sprays are good for the house. Yard sprays are effective for lawns and outdoor runs. Hire a professional exterminator if necessary.

Look for fleas on your Lhasa around the tail, head, back, belly, and rear legs. If no fleas are seen, check for "flea dirt" which is tiny black particles of dried blood and flea feces. Many types of products are available to rid your dog of fleas, including shampoos, dips, collars, powders, and sprays. There is even a tablet available to give your Lhasa that kills fleas when they bite your dog. Check with your veterinarian for the most effective products in your area because fleas in some areas have developed resistance to common insecticides. He or she can also recommend a flea-control program best suited for your particular circumstances.

Ticks

Ticks are most active in the summer months and are generally found in wooded, tall, grassy areas. They firmly attach themselves by embedding their mouthparts into the dog's skin. Ticks feed on blood and become engorged, increasing in size many times over.

Heavy infestations can cause a serious blood loss (anemia). Ticks can also transmit serious diseases to dogs, such as Babesia (a blood parasite) and tick paralysis.

To remove a tick, first place a drop of alcohol or insecticide around the head of the tick, then wait for a moment. Grasp the head of the tick with tweezers as close to the skin as possible and pull with firm, steady pressure, making sure to get all the mouth parts. Disinfect the skin with alcohol after removal of the tick.

Tick infestations are best controlled by insecticide dips which are poured or sprayed on your dog's coat and allowed to dry. When dipping at home always strictly follow directions on the label or leave the application to your veterinarian or professional groomer.

Note: In some areas of the United States tick bites can transmit very serious diseases to humans, such as Rocky Mountain Spotted Fever, Lyme disease, and tularemia. Symptoms include fever, muscle pain, and skin rashes. Consult your physician immediately if you have any of these symptoms.

Lice

Dogs are rarely infested with lice. If present, the hair coat will be rough and dry and in heavy infestations may be matted. Look for adult lice and their eggs (called nits) attached to hair on the neck, tail, head, and the ears. Repeated insecticide treatments are necessary to kill the eggs as they hatch. Dog lice do not infest humans.

Ear mites

These mites are found in your dog's ear canal and can only be seen with magnification. They cause a dark, gritty, and waxy build-up in the outer ear canal and are easily transmitted to other dogs and cats when they come in contact with each other. If your Lhasa is shaking its head or scratching its ears, your veterinarian can examine the ears with an otoscope and if mites are found may prescribe medication for you to put in your dog's ears.

Mange

There are two types of mange, demodectic (red mange) and sarcoptic (scabies). Both are caused by mites.

Medical Care for Your Lhasa

Demodex Mites live in the dog's hair follicles, causing patchy hair loss and secondary infection. Dogs may or may not itch. The severity of the disease can vary greatly. Puppies and old dogs are most susceptible. Fortunately, demodectic mange is not contagious to other dogs or humans.

When a Lhasa is affected with demodectic mange, it is best to clip its hair short (about ½ inch [1.3 cm]). This makes the necessary bathing and dipping much easier. It also increases the effectiveness of the treatment.

Sarcoptes Mites burrow into the skin, causing hair loss and skin irritation. Dogs are usually extremely itchy. These mites are highly contagious to other animals and can temporarily infest people.

Professional help is needed to diagnose and effectively treat mange. Your veterinarian may want to take skin scrapings from your dog and examine them under a microscope to detect and differentiate these mites. Appropriate therapy can then be instituted.

Common Medical Problems

Scratching and Hair Loss

If your Lhasa suddenly starts scratching itself, first check for external parasites such as fleas (see page 37). They can also cause hair loss and skin irritation. If none are seen or your dog continues to scratch despite flea treatment, your pet may have allergies or mange (scabies) (see page 38).

If your Lhasa is losing hair but is not particularly itchy, nutritional imbalances, hormone deficiencies, ringworm, and demodex (see page 39) are all possible causes.

If scratching or hair loss persists, see your veterinarian. Many of these conditions respond well to treatment after a specific diagnosis is made.

Vomiting and Diarrhea

Occasional vomiting or loose stool usually is not serious. A change in diet, stress or excitement, or getting into the garbage can cause your Lhasa to vomit or have diarrhea. Intestinal parasites commonly produce these symptoms in puppies.

These problems can be serious if the vomiting or diarrhea is severe or persists more than 12 to 24 hours. For instructions and dietary management, see page 48.

Constipation

If your Lhasa has not had a bowel movement recently and is straining to defecate, he or she may be constipated. Ingestion of bones is a common cause of constipation. Mineral oil (1 teaspoon per 10 pounds [4-5 kg] of body weight) or a children's dose of metamucil may be added to the food. If no improvement is seen in a day or two or if your pet is in obvious discomfort, call your veterinarian.

Scooting

When a dog "scoots" along the floor on its bottom, this is usually the result of impaction of the anal sacs, allergies, or a tapeworm infection.

The anal sacs are two glands that lie under the skin, one on each side of the anus. They produce a strong, musty smelling, thick fluid. Sometimes dogs are unable to express the fluid from the anal sacs, resulting in anal sac impaction and irritation. Your veterinarian can check these glands and evacuate them if necessary.

Tapeworms can be identified in the stool or around the anus (see page 36). If allergies are responsible for the scooting, the tail head and area around the anus will be red and irritated. Medication is available from your veterinarian.

Eyes and Ears

Occasional matter in the corner of your Lhasa's eyes is of no great concern. Gently wipe matter from the corner of the eye with a lint-free cloth or facial tissue. However, if the discharge from the eyes is excessive or if the eyes are red and your dog is squinting and showing obvious discomfort, let your veterinarian examine the eyes. Sometimes

Medical Care for Your Lhasa

Administering medication is an important technique to master. Open the jaws as shown here by placing your thumb and index finger behind the upper canines.

Place the tablet back as far in the mouth as possible. Gently hold mouth shut until the tablet is swallowed.

foreign bodies such as hair, eyelashes, or small grass seeds are found irritating the eyes. Excessive nasal skin folds may rub against the eyes causing serious eye irritation. Surgical correction may be necessary.

As your Lhasa gets older you may notice the eyes becoming "cloudy." This is probably due to cataract formation. Cataracts occur when the lens inside the eye becomes opaque. Eventually they can impair vision.

If your dog's ears are inflamed, sore to the touch, or have a strong odor and discharge they need urgent attention. If not treated promptly, serious middle ear and inner ear infections can result. Your veterinarian will examine your dog's ear canals with an otoscope and may prescribe an appropriate medication for you to apply at home. With your Lhasa under anesthesia, severe infections and waxy impactions in the ear may require cleaning and flushing at your doctor's clinic.

The old adage "An ounce of prevention is worth a pound of cure" is never truer than with regard to the eyes and ears. For proper cleaning and maintenance of the eyes and ears, see section under grooming.

It is beyond the scope of this book to describe every conceivable medical problem your Lhasa may encounter in his or her life. As owner and caretaker of your pet it is your responsibility to keep your Lhasa as healthy as possible by recognizing problems and seeking professional medical attention when needed. Below are a list of symptoms that should alert you to health problems in your Lhasa apso. If any of these symptoms persist for more than 12 to 24 hours call your veterinarian. If your dog is in pain or symptoms seem to be getting worse don't wait 24 hours. Use your common sense and good judgement. Also refer to sections on emergencies.

• listlessness, depression
• abnormal breathing
• coughing
• discharge from nose
• increase or decrease in thirst or appetite

Medical Care for Your Lhasa

An otoscope aids the veterinarian in examining deep inside the external ear canal.

- vomiting, diarrhea
- straining to urinate
- urinating frequently
- fever (greater than 103°F [39.4°C])
- limping
- back or neck pain
- bloat
- discharge from vulva or penis

Obesity

Obesity is the most common and most preventable problem occurring in dogs today. The American Animal Hospital Association estimates that 40% of all dogs in the United States are affected. Overweight dogs develop more health problems and generally don't live as long as trim dogs. They suffer many of the same problems overweight people experience—heart and vascular disease, bone and joint ailments, diabetes and skin ailments.

A dog becomes overweight when his food intake exceeds his energy requirements. Older dogs are especially prone to obesity because they become less active, hence their energy needs decrease, yet they continue to eat as much as they used to eat when they were younger. Keep in mind that an adult Lhasa normally weighs between 15 to 20 pounds, so a 5-pound weight gain is very significant.

If you suspect your Lhasa is overweight, be sure and have your dog examined by a veterinarian. There are certain genetic, metabolic, and hormonal imbalances that will cause obesity. Your doctor can decide if these problems are responsible for the weight gain and also determine if any other medical problems are developing.

There are two simple ways to reduce your dog's weight—by diet and exercise. You can put your dog on a specific reducing diet or just feed less of what he or she normally eats. Your veterinarian can give you guidelines as to the type of food and how much to feed.

Exercise will help your dog burn excess calories. It will also strengthen his heart and lungs and increase his muscle tone. Start gradually and slowly increase his exercise. Walking is an easy and simple way to exercise your dog. Start slowly, as an overweight dog tires easily.

Old Age

When your Lhasa apso reaches about eight or nine years of age you may begin to notice changes beginning to take place in his or her behavior, activity level, and physical stature.

Your pet may begin to slow down, sleep more, and generally become less active. He or she may develop problems with urination or bowel movements. Teeth and gums will require more attention due to accumulation of plaque and tartar on the teeth. The hair coat may become thinner, the skin less supple, and warts and other skin growths may appear. Cataracts become visible and hearing may diminish. These are all signs of the ageing process. Arthritis, kidney, and heart disease may develop as your dog gets older. This is not to imply that every

Medical Care for Your Lhasa

dog will have all these ailments. Your dog may not skip a beat until 15 years of age. But it is important to recognize problems and prepare yourself for these changes. Fortunately, if recognized early, many of these ailments can be managed satisfactorily for a long time. Regular checkups by your veterinarian are especially important as your dog gets older. He or she can recognize early signs of illness and advise you on preventive care and dietary modifications.

Euthanasia

Unfortunately, there may come a time when the natural ageing process or a terminal disease will start to profoundly affect your pet. The quality of its life will deteriorate to the point where there is little joy in life. Even the most basic functions such as eating, walking, and eliminating may become difficult to accomplish without pain or intensive care. At this point euthanasia should be considered. Dis-

cuss the situation with your veterinarian thoroughly. He or she can provide you with a professional opinion about the probabilities of improvement and the quality of life your dog can expect. Ultimately the decision rests with the pet owner. It is not an easy decision when we've had a faithful companion for many years, but sometimes it is more humane to spare a pet needless pain and suffering.

Euthanasia is painless and humane. Your veterinarian will inject a solution similar to an anesthetic into the dog's vein and he will quickly fall asleep, dying peacefully and with dignity.

The bond we establish with our pets is a very strong one. Our pet easily becomes a member of the family. Therefore, it is natural to experience feelings of emptiness, sadness, and bereavement. Try to focus on all the love and companionship that was shared over the years together and realize that with pet ownership comes responsibility, and that responsibility includes preventing pointless pain and suffering.

Emergency Care and First Aid

When confronted with an emergency, above all, try to remain calm. By applying basic first-aid techniques your Lhasa's life may be saved. It is equally important to be able to recognize a true emergency so that immediate veterinary attention can be sought. Don't hesitate to call your veterinarian for advice if needed.

Accidents

If your Lhasa has been injured and is in pain approach your pet with extreme caution. Your normally loving pet may behave unpredictably, even bite, when it is in pain. If a muzzle is needed a piece of cloth, a rope, or a necktie may be used. First form a loop around the mouth and tie the muzzle shut. Then loop the ends under the jaw and pass them around the back of the head behind the ears and tie it fairly snug.

Next wrap or roll your pet in a towel or blanket or other material to act as a stretcher. Gently place your dog in your car and get immediate veterinary attention. A call to your vet to notify him or her of your emergency is helpful so that the doctor can prepare for your animal.

Bleeding

First, identify where your dog is bleeding. Many times dogs will lick at the area of bleeding. Apply direct pressure with a compress over the bleeding site. If bleeding can't be controlled with direct pressure, a tourniquet may be applied if the wound is on the leg or tail. Be sure and loosen the tourniquet every 15 minutes to relieve pressure and allow circulation. A nosebleed can be controlled by elevating the head and applying a cold compress to the nose. Notify your veterinarian if bleeding persists or if significant blood loss has occurred.

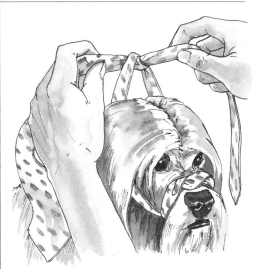

In an emergency, a tie can be fashioned into an effective muzzle. It should be tied snugly, but not too tightly.

Convulsions

Convulsions (seizures) are rarely fatal and don't usually last more than a minute or two. Avoid getting your face or hands near the dog's mouth because a seizuring dog usually does not know what it is doing and may bite accidentally. Your veterinarian can help determine the cause of seizuring. Medication may be needed if seizuring is frequent.

Poisoning

If your Lhasa has been poisoned, first identify the poison. This is very important for treatment as antidotes are available for certain types of poisons. Call your veterinarian and be prepared to bring in the container of poison. The exact ingredients may

Emergency Care and First Aid

Common Types of Poison

POISON	IMMEDIATE TREATMENT IF POISON IS KNOWN	FOUND IN	SYMPTOMS	COMMENTS
Insecticides	If on skin wash with mild soap	Dips, flea sprays, pest-control chemicals	Vomiting, diarrhea, salivating, seizures	Usually a result of combining flea treatments or not diluting solutions properly
Warfarin	None, no home treatment effective	Rat and mouse bait	Red patches on skin and gums, bleeding from body openings in severe cases	Symptoms may not be present for 2–3 days after ingestion
Ethylene Glycol	* Induce vomiting	Antifreeze	Incoordination, vomiting, lack of urine output	Very deadly, must start antidote immediately; causes severe kidney damage. *Do not wait* for symptoms to appear.
Arsenic	* Induce vomiting	Ant poisons, insecticides, herbicides	Vomiting, diarrhea, abdominal pain, restlessness	
Phosphorus	* Induce vomiting	Rat poisons, fireworks, "strike anywhere" matches	Vomiting (garlic odor), diarrhea, abdominal pain	

* Vomiting may be induced by administering 1–2 tsp. hydrogen peroxide or 1 tsp. table salt orally. Save vomitus. Do not induce vomiting if acid, alkali, or other caustic material has been ingested.

Above: With proper training, Lhasas can learn a variety of commands. This Lhasa is learning to heel without a leash. Below: This playful Lhasa is shown retrieving a barbell.

Emergency Care and First Aid

be needed to treat your pet successfully. Poison-control centers are available to you and your doctor for consultation if needed.

Bites and Stings

Superficial bite wounds should be gently washed with soap and water and disinfected with hydrogen peroxide. Larger lacerations and muscle tears will require stitches. Deep puncture wounds can easily cause infection. Consult your veterinarian.

Insect stings can be painful and usually occur in the face or paws. They may cause redness and swelling. If swelling persists or if your Lhasa has an allergic reaction to stings (difficult breathing, vomiting, hives, or facial swelling) call your veterinarian without delay.

Snakebites usually cause bleeding at the puncture sites followed by severe swelling and intense pain. Take your dog to the veterinarian without delay.

Heat Stroke

Heat stroke is very dangerous and can quickly lead to death. Heat stroke is usually caused by high temperature and poor ventilation such as is caused by leaving a dog in a locked car in the summertime. Lhasas can also overheat by exercising vigorously in high temperature with no water available.

Symptoms of heat stroke include high fever, very rapid, shallow panting, and a blank expression. The gums are usually bright red. This is a life-threatening situation. Immediately sponge your dog's entire body with cool water or with a mixture of cool water and alcohol. Then rush your pet to the veterinary hospital.

Lhasas will enjoy all the attention their owners can give them. Above: This little fellow is eager to demonstrate his prowess at fetching. Below: Regular exercise is necessary for maintaining the health and well-being of any dog. This Lhasa is enjoying a stroll through the woods.

Never leave your Lhasa in an unattended car on a warm day, even with the windows partially rolled down! Temperatures can rise in a very short time, causing heat stroke.

Emergency Care and First Aid

Vomiting and Diarrhea

If your Lhasa is vomiting frequently and profusely, withhold food and water. When the vomiting has subsided, offer small quantities of water only, every 30 minutes. If the dog is keeping the water down, bland food such as lean chicken and rice may be given in small amounts until the dog appears normal.

With diarrhea, withhold food for several hours but allow your dog water at all times. Small amounts of a bland diet may then be offered. Gradually over two to three days change back to your dog's regular food.

If there is any blood in the vomitus or stool, or if the condition continues for more than 12 to 24 hours, contact your veterinarian.

Eye Injuries

Any traumatic injury to the eye is always dangerous. Your pet's eyes should be examined by your veterinarian immediately.

If soap or other caustic substances get into the eyes, flush the eyes with eye wash or tap water. If redness, tearing, or squinting of the eyes persist, seek veterinary attention.

Behavior and Training

In order to understand your Lhasa's behavior and develop a good relationship with him, it is helpful to consider where dogs came from and how they evolved. Dogs' ancestors were similar to the present-day wolf. Wolves are pack animals and have a well-developed social organization within each pack. The leader of each pack is called the "alpha" wolf. This alpha wolf is the dominant individual in the pack. He settles disputes and offers guidance for younger members of the pack. All other individuals are subordinate to him. Through their heirarchy, individuals in the pack feel secure and tensions between individuals are reduced.

Your Lhasa is also a pack animal. He sees you and members of your household as his pack. His source of security is now people in the household rather than other dogs. In your pet's eyes you are now the alpha leader. This is a very important point in establishing a healthy, pleasant, and long-lasting relationship with your Lhasa. You are his master and he looks to you for guidance. He will feel secure and will be eager to please you if he clearly understands his pecking order in the household and his relationship with you. Problems develop when the dog is allowed to assume the dominant role and his master is now subordinate to him. This does not mean that you must be cruel or abusive to a pet to assert a leadership position. Your dog will be a more enjoyable pet and a happier dog if it knows what is expected of him and is treated in a consistent and positive fashion.

Essentials of Training

A well-trained dog is a joy to be with and is a great companion. Training your Lhasa will be a source of satisfaction for both you and your pet. A well-trained dog tends to be better adjusted and a more appreciated member of the household. Keep in mind that training is more than giving commands and following orders. It involves developing an at-

titude of respect and admiration between dog and owner, which will give your Lhasa a sense of security and belonging. He will then know and appreciate his place in the household "pack."

How does one go about successfully training a Lhasa apso? First, approach training from your dog's point of view. Remember, you are the leader of his pack and he seeks your approval for his behavior. Second, every dog is an individual. Training techniques may need to be tailored to your dog's personality. For instance a very shy, submissive dog requires a gentle, calm, reassuring voice, whereas a dominant, strong-willed dog needs a firm, unwavering tone that conveys authority. There are many different methods of successfully training dogs. I encourage you to read about different training techniques. This will allow you to select methods you are most comfortable with and that are appropriate for your situation.

Regardless of the particular training method used, here are some basic suggestions that will improve your training skills.

Your Lhasa will respond to lots of praise and affection for a job well done.

49

Behavior and Training

Praise: Praise and positive reinforcement are the cornerstones of successful training. Praise is such a powerful tool because most dogs thrive on a show of approval. Praise should be both verbal and physical. Pet your dog and talk to him in a positive, reassuring tone. The amount and kind of praise should be appropriate for the situation. For instance, if you are teaching your dog to sit and you lavishly praise him when he sits, he may get so excited that he jumps around and forgets all about sitting. Praise should be more than just a reward for proper behavior. Base your relationship with your Lhasa on a positive, upbeat attitude. By establishing this attitude, simply withholding praise and voicing displeasure may be all the discipline necessary when your dog misbehaves.

Treats: Motivating your dog using praise will also decrease the need for using treats as a reward. Treats are all right for a reward if given *occasionally*. Give them only after a specific task or command has been completed. Never give treats after unwanted behavior or simply to pacify your pet. Remember, treats add calories to your dog's diet and can contribute to obesity.

Patience: Training takes time and repetition. Never scream at your dog or lose your temper. A stern "no" or "bad dog" will communicate your displeasure if he misbehaves. Keep training sessions short and enthusiastic, especially with puppies. Ten to fifteen minutes of training two or three times daily is plenty.

Consistency: You must be consistent in defining acceptable and nonacceptable behavior. It's confusing to your pet if you allow him to jump up on you but not on your guests. Consistency is also important in your training sessions. Use the same words and voice inflections for each training exercise. When your pet understands that what is expected of him today was the same as yesterday and will be the same tomorrow, you've accomplished your goal, namely acceptable, repeatable behavior.

Be Clear: Make sure you and your pet have a clear understanding of what you want to accomplish. Also your commands and gestures should be clear and unambiguous. When your dog misbehaves, make eye contact and follow with a firm "no!" making certain that you convey your displeasure. Praise or reprimands should be given immediately after the actions that warranted a response. It is confusing to a dog to scold him for a mistake that was made an hour earlier.

Attention: There is no substitute for simply spending time with your pet. For most dogs, the greatest reward is their master giving them lots of love and attention. Pet them, hug them, rub them, and give them positive encouragement. You will have a lifelong friend who gives you unconditional affection. Play time, apart from formal training sessions, is necessary to establish a healthy pet-owner bond.

On the other hand, lack of attention will encourage bad habits and destructive behavior. Many times when dogs chew the furniture or dig holes in the yard it is due to boredom or a lack of attention. For some dogs negative attention is better than no attention at all. The scolding they get for misbehaving is the only attention they are receiving.

Discipline

No caring dog owner ever enjoys disciplining his or her pet. However, there are instances when discipline is necessary. Many times verbal scolding is essential to convey displeasure. A stern "no" or "bad dog" is necessary to proclaim unacceptable behavior. Make sure your tone of voice is firm and unwavering, asserting clear authority. Physical discipline is sometimes necessary for unruly dogs if proper techniques are used. This does not mean beating your dog with a stick or newspaper. One effective technique is to grab the dog by the scruff of the neck and shake him. Be sure to scold him verbally at the same time. For serious breaches of behavior turn the dog over on his back, holding him by the scruff of his neck, and verbally reprimand him. This places the dog in a very submissive posture.

Rules for Effective Discipline

• Never call your Lhasa to you and then discipline him. You should go get the dog, but do not chase him. His name and the command to come should always be in a positive tone.
• Discipline immediately after misbehavior. Your dog will not understand why he is being punished if there is a long period between misbehavior and punishment.
• Make eye contact with your Lhasa. You will know you have his attention and he will not be easily distracted.
• Do not start playing with your Lhasa immediately after disciplining; remain passive for a few minutes.

Obedience Classes

Whether your Lhasa is easy to train or you're having problems, you should consider obedience classes. There you will learn sound, proper techniques and will get instructions and practice on a regular basis. It also provides good socialization for your dog to become accustomed to other people and animals. Most schools have classes for puppies and older dogs. You will probably need a health and vaccination certificate to enroll in the class.

If you are having serious problems with your dog, such as biting, aggressiveness, or chronic housesoiling, etc., you may want to seek a private trainer who will work with you individually.

Check with your veterinarian or local dog clubs for reputable trainers and obedience schools. Ask your friends who have completed obedience classes about their experiences with their trainer and his or her effectiveness.

Housebreaking

There is nothing mysterious about housebreaking your Lhasa apso. Most puppies are relatively easy to train to eliminate where you want them to, provided you are patient, consistent, and follow some commonsense rules. Here are some guidelines to help you:
• Make sure your dog has firm stools, is free of intestinal parasites, and is generally healthy. If a dog is straining to urinate or has diarrhea and must go frequently, it may prove to be almost impossible to housebreak him.
• Start your puppy on a good-quality dog food. Avoid table scraps and treats.
• Establish regular feeding times. As soon as your puppy finishes eating there is a natural urge to eliminate. Use this to your advantage. After feeding, take your puppy out to the desired toilet area. Stay with him until he eliminates. Praise him lavishly for his good behavior. Do *not* leave food out for him to nibble on throughout the day while he is being housebroken because it will be harder to gauge when he has to go out. Three to four feedings per day is sufficient for most puppies. This can be reduced to one to two feedings per day for an adult dog. Water may be left down all day if housebreaking is proceeding smoothly. If you are having any difficulty, offer water at regular intervals only and take up the water at night.
• Encourage your dog to eliminate in only one area. When dogs can smell where they have gone previously it will trigger them to repeat in the same spot.
• Anticipate when your puppy has to relieve himself. Take him out after feeding, drinking, taking a nap, awakening in the morning, and playing with toys. Learn to recognize when your puppy has to go out. The telltale signs include squatting, sniffing, walking in a circle, or loitering at the door. If he starts to go, startle him with a loud noise or clap and simply take him to the desired area and praise him when he finishes eliminating. Never scold him

at the site where he is supposed to go. He needs positive reinforcement there, not punishment.

• If you find a mistake in the house, do not rub the dog's nose in it. Not only is this unsanitary, it will send the wrong signal to your dog. Don't make a big fuss over it. If your dog sees the mistake, growl and scowl at him and take him out to his toilet area. Do not let your dog see you clean up the accident. You can neutralize the odor with 25% white vinegar and water or odor neutralizers.

• Puppies are inherently clean and don't want to soil their own den. For this reason it is best to accustom your puppy to sleeping in a small crate or box. When you're away from home during the day, confine him to one room of the house, particularly one with vinyl or linoleum floors. If you want your dog to eliminate outside, skip paper-training him inside. This only teaches him it's all right to go inside and prolongs the whole housebreaking process. You may, however, need to paper-train your dog if you live in a highrise apartment or if it is difficult to take your dog out regularly. The training method is the same as outside training.

Basic Commands

Many people make the mistake of waiting too long to begin obedience training. If you don't begin early you'll have to break the bad habits your Lhasa has already developed before you can teach him correct behavior. Before training begins you'll need to purchase a collar and leash (see page 16). A training (choke) collar made of stainless steel or nylon with smooth action provides good control for correcting behavior immediately. You can begin simple obedience training when your Lhasa reaches eight to ten weeks of age. Let him get used to the collar and leash before working with him. Under direct supervision, let him wander around the house with his leash attached to his collar for a few minutes each day. In no time at all your Lhasa will

consider the collar and leash just a minor inconvenience. When teaching basic commands there is one point I want to emphasize. If your dog is not on a leash and needs to be scolded for misbehaving in any way, go to your dog to reprimand him. Never call your Lhasa to come and then punish him when he arrives. The command to come when called is perhaps the most important command to learn. It may save his life someday if he wanders toward a busy street. When your Lhasa obeys you and comes when called he should always be rewarded with praise. Always make it a positive experience.

Heel

As soon as your Lhasa is accustomed to having his collar and leash on, you can teach him to heel. Teaching your dog to heel is not only useful, it's satisfying to know your dog will stay with you, neither lunging ahead nor following behind when you're out for a stroll.

One of the first commands to teach your Lhasa is to heel. Use quick, deliberate motions and an authoritative voice. Position your Lhasa on your left side, maintaining a short leash for instant corrective action.

Behavior and Training

The "sit" command. Push your Lhasa's hind quarters down while using the other hand to keep it's head up and facing front.

Sit

Position your Lhasa on your left side and hold the leash in your right hand. Push his rump down with your left hand while simultaneously pulling his head up with the leash. Give him the command "Sit" while he goes through the motions. When he's in the sitting position shower him with praise. Repeat the exercise until your Lhasa will sit without his rump being forced down. Evenetually he should learn to sit by voice command only, without his leash being used or having to be touched. Initially, don't make him sit too long or he'll get restless. Keep the training sessions short, especially if your Lhasa is young. He'll progress faster with short exercises three or four times daily than with one long training period. Don't be discouraged if there are setbacks and mistakes. Remember, patience, repetition, and persistence will pay off in the long run.

To begin, position your Lhasa on your left side. As you step out with your left foot, say "Heel" quickly with authority. You may also say your dog's name when giving the command to heel. If he doesn't start walking when you do, snap the leash, say "Heel" and his name, and start walking again. If he runs ahead quickly, make a 90-degree turn to the right, telling him to heel as the leash pulls tight. You shouldn't be in a tug of war. Motions should be quick. Offer encouragement and praise frequently as he improves. Don't expect everything to go smoothly at first. Your Lhasa will jump around, tug at the leash, or decide he's had enough of this and put the brakes on and refuse to budge. Try always to end the training sessions on an upbeat, positive note. Eventually, he should learn to sit whenever you come to a stop. Just remember that once your Lhasa gets the hang of it, he'll eagerly look forward to his next outing.

Repetition and praise for performing well is the best way to teach your dog the "stay." As you practice, gradually increase the distance and length of time you maintain the command.

Behavior and Training

Stay

Once you have taught your Lhasa how to sit you've already crossed half the bridge of teaching him to stay. With your Lhasa sitting at your left, hold his head up with the leash if necessary. Moving your right foot first, direct your left hand in front of your Lhasa's face. Your hand should be open with your fingers together and your palm facing your pet. Say "Stay" in a firm authoritative tone as you turn directly in front of your Lhasa so he is unable to move forward. At first just make him hold the stay for a few seconds, then give him an upbeat, positive signal such as "good boy" or "okay" to let him know it's all right to move.

Once he learns to stay when you're right in front of him, gradually step back further, until you can be out of sight and your Lhasa will hold the stay. If he breaks the stay, make him sit and emphasize the stay command by pushing both hands in front of him.

Come

The two most important ingredients for being successful in getting your Lhasa to come when called is to be enthusiastic and always make it a positive experience for your pet. Call your dog by his name and say "Come." Crouch down to his level and welcome him with open arms. Make eye contact with him and let him know you're glad to see him. Pet him and give him lots of praise. If you need to, start training him with a leash by giving it a tug when you call him. As I've said before, never scold your Lhasa after he's come when called. Nobody wants to come to someone if they think they'll be punished when they get there.

Breeding Lhasas

If you are thinking about breeding your Lhasa, please take the time to consider thoroughly if you are willing to commit the necessary time, effort, and expense needed to produce and raise a litter of puppies. Sure, Lhasa puppies are adorable, cute, little furry creatures. Breeding dogs can be an educational and very rewarding experience. However, you have a responsibility to the breed and future owners of the puppies to produce healthy, good-quality, even-tempered Lhasas of which you can be proud. If you think breeding will be a big money-making proposition, you may be disappointed. Stud fees, feed costs, deworming, vaccinations—not to mention what your time is worth—will all take a bite out of the profit margin. Selling puppies is not always an easy task. And there is no truth to the notion that a female will benefit psychologically or physically as a result of producing a litter.

If you decide to breed your Lhasa, you'll enjoy the whole experience even more if you know what to expect and set goals to produce good-quality Lhasas. To gain knowledge, talk to experienced breeders and consult with your veterinarian. Learn as much about the breed as possible.

If you decide not to breed your female Lhasa, give serious consideration to having her spayed. Many people who want to have their dog spayed think they have to wait until after their dog comes into season the first time. This is an old wives tale that has no basis in fact. Actually, spaying a bitch before her first heat period greatly reduces her chances of developing breast cancer later in life.

The Female Estrus Cycle

The bitch (female) will come in season (estrus) approximately every six months. Her first estrus cycle or heat period begins usually when she is six to eight months of age. There can be some variation in these time frames. It's best not to breed the bitch until her third heat. This allows time for her own development into adulthood and gives you the opportunity to determine if she is cycling normally.

The first sign of your Lhasa coming into season will be swelling of the vulva and concurrent blood-tinged vaginal discharge. This early bleeding phase lasts about seven to ten days. During this time, males will be attracted to the female but she will not be receptive nor would she be able to conceive because she has not yet ovulated. The next phase in the estrus cycle is the true heat period called estrus. The bitch has ovulated, meaning the ova (eggs) have ripened and are ready for fertilization. This is also referred to as "standing heat" because the bitch will be receptive to the male and will allow him to mount her. The vaginal discharge usually subsides and turns clear. The bitch will remain in estrus for about four to seven days during which time fertilization can occur. If she does not become pregnant, the ova degenerate, and she enters a dormant phase until her next cycle begins all over again.

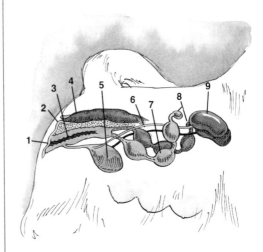

The female reproductive system.
1. vulva 2. anus 3. vagina 4. rectum 5. bladder 6. ureter 7. developing embryo 8. ovaries 9. kidney

Breeding Lhasas

False Pregnancy

Occasionally a bitch will not actually be pregnant but will exhibit all the signs of pregnancy. Her breasts enlarge and she may even produce milk. As the imaginary whelping date approaches she'll be restless and might fashion a den. You'll swear she is carrying a litter of puppies even though she wasn't bred or wasn't even near a male for that matter. This is a false pregnancy and is caused by a hormonal imbalance in the bitch. False pregnancies occur after the heat period and last 40 to 65 days. This phenomenon usually resolves on its own and treatment is rarely necessary.

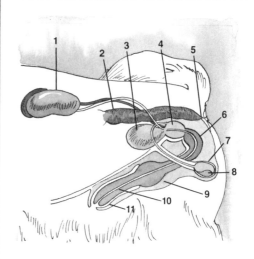

The male reproductive system.
1. kidneys 2. rectum 3. bladder 4. prostate 5. anus 6. urethra 7. scrotum 8. testes 9. bulb 10. penis 11. sheath

The Stud

It's wise to begin looking for the ideal mate well before the anticipated breeding dates. You may be able to find a perfectly acceptable sire locally or if you're very discriminating and want a particular champion show dog, your search may take you clear across the country.

Regardless of whether your breeding goals are show or pet-quality puppies, the overall criteria for choosing a stud are the same. A healthy sire with no birth defects or hereditary illnesses will be more likely to produce puppies of similar healthy stature. Of course not all hereditary traits will be manifested every generation. For this reason it's a good idea to check out the potential sire's pedigree. The more you know about the sire's background the easier it will be to assess his desirabilities as a stud. Good sources for finding a stud are local and national dog clubs, veterinarians, and dog magazines.

The sire should be at least one year old and preferably experienced. The mating will go much smoother with an "old pro"—i.e., don't send a boy in to do a man's job! Since the male is more comfortable on his own turf, the bitch is usually brought to the male for breeding. Many breeders will require a test for the male and female to make sure they are free of brucellosis. Brucellosis is a bacterial disease that can be transmitted venereally and may cause abortions and sterility.

The stud-fee arrangements should be clearly understood by both parties. Generally, the stud fee is the value of a puppy, or some stud owners might request the pick of the litter as payment.

Mating

Make sure your bitch is in top condition before she is due to come in season. She should be trim and exhibit good muscle tone. If your female is too fat or too thin, it will be more difficult for her to conceive. Before breeding her, take her to your veterinarian so he or she can examine her, check her

Breeding Lhasas

for worms, and make sure your Lhasa is up to date on her vaccinations.

The correct time to mate the bitch is when she is in true estrus (ovulating). How do we know when she is in estrus? Fortunately, we can let nature take its course—the female will usually only let the male mount her when she is in estrus. When the bitch is ready she'll welcome his advances by standing for him and moving her tail to one side, thus exposing her vulva. A general rule of thumb is to allow breeding on the tenth and twelfth days of the heat period in which day one is the first sign of bloody vaginal discharge.

During normal copulation the male and female may be locked together for several minutes. This is referred to as the "tie." Do not try to separate them. They will separate naturally as sexual tension subsides. If it's difficult to determine when your bitch is ready to breed, consult your veterinarian. He or she can determine ideal breeding dates by microscopically evaluating cells from the genital tract. Artificial insemination is also commonly employed when natural breeding is unsuccessful.

If your female has been bred, be sure to keep her away from other males. I still remember how surprised one of my clients was when she brought in a litter of cocker spaniel puppies for an exam. She was puzzled because the puppies "looked so different." Half of the litter looked like cocker spaniels and the other half were mongrels. You can imagine the expression on my client's face when she was told her bitch had been serviced by two different males!

Pregnancy

If all goes well, your Lhasa will give birth nine weeks after conception. Sixty-three days is average, although this can vary somewhat. The bitch will not look much different until she is five to six weeks pregnant. At this time you may notice her abdomen becoming more pendulous and her breasts

and nipples growing in size. Approximately one week before whelping she'll start producing milk. By feeling individual embryos in the womb, your veterinarian can sometimes determine if your Lhasa is pregnant at 21 to 30 days gestation.

It is important not to overfeed your Lhasa when she is pregnant. If she's overweight at whelping time, she's more likely to experience difficulty delivering the puppies. She will gradually increase her food intake the first six weeks. The last two to three weeks you'll notice a big increase in her appetite. She needs more to eat during the last trimester because embryos are growing rapidly. Be sure your Lhasa is eating a high-quality dog food that is complete and balanced. Ask your veterinarian for advice before giving any vitamin and mineral supplements. Your Lhasa will receive more vitamins and minerals simply by increasing her food intake.

Whelping

Two to three weeks before the whelping date get your Lhasa accustomed to a whelping box. The box should be just large enough for your bitch to lay down in comfortably. Ideally, the sides of the whelping box should be a few inches tall to keep the puppies from wandering, yet low enough to allow the mother to come and go as she pleases. A cozy den-like whelping box will help make the mother feel secure and relaxed. Place the whelping box away from drafts in a quiet room with minimal foot traffic. A spare bedroom or even a closet is a good choice. Encourage your Lhasa to nap and sleep in the box at night so she is familiar with it by delivery time. A soft towel placed in the box for bedding would also be appreciated by your Lhasa.

As the delivery day approaches, the bitch may become restless and uncomfortable. She'll probably rearrange the bedding material in the whelping box. It's a good idea at this time to clip the hair around the vulva to facilitate cleanliness.

It is interesting to note that an expectant fe-

Breeding Lhasas

male's temperature will drop about 24 hours before delivery. Use a rectal thermometer and start taking her temperature twice daily a few days before her due date. A dog's normal temperature is 101° to 102°F (38.3°–38.9°C). Approximately 24 hours before whelping, your Lhasa's temperature will fall below 100°F (37.8°C). It is also not unusual for the female to refuse food 12 to 24 hours before whelping.

Fortunately, giving birth to puppies is a natural process that usually requires minimal intervention. However, if you're prepared for the unexpected and can react to any difficulties quickly you can save a little puppy's life should a problem develop. For reasons I'll mention, I recommend being present for your Lhasa's whelping.

As labor begins the bitch usually starts panting and appears restless. This early stage of labor may last several hours. When your Lhasa starts having forceful abdominal contractions and is obviously straining, this is referred to as hard labor. If a puppy is not born within three hours after the onset of hard labor, contact your veterinarian immediately for advice. The interval between the birth of the puppies can also vary from between a few minutes to several hours. If the bitch is comfortable and not straining or in pain, everything is probably all right. Again, if she's in hard labor, a puppy should be delivered within three hours. If not, consult your veterinarian. Sometimes the mother becomes exhausted or has other difficulties that prevent her from delivering normally. If medications fail to help, your veterinarian may need to perform a cesarean section. In this surgical procedure the puppies are removed from the womb via an incision into the abdomen.

In the womb each puppy is surrounded by a placental sac that supplies it with nourishment. Many times the sac ruptures before the puppy is born, liberating the fluid into the birth canal. If the fetal membranes still surround the puppy when it's born, the mother should tear them away and begin licking and cleaning the puppy. This licking action will literally bring the puppy to life by stimulating the new-born puppy to take its first breath of air and begin normal breathing. After cleaning the puppy, the bitch will routinely eat the placental membranes (afterbirth). In the process she will sever the umbilical cord. The puppies instinctively seek the mother's nipples and begin nursing shortly after birth.

If the mother fails to tear the membranes and free the puppy from the sac, you should step in immediately and assist her. After cleaning away the fetal membranes, open the puppy's mouth and clear its throat by removing any mucus or fluid present. Next, stimulate its breathing by rubbing the puppy with a towel. This simulates the licking and cleaning action of the mother. One reason I recommend always attending your Lhasa's delivery is because due to their undershot jaw they may have difficulty severing the umbilical cord. As a result they tear off the cord too close to the puppy's body and create an umbilical hernia. This can easily be avoided by cutting the cord with a blunt pair of scissors (disinfect in alcohol first), leaving the cord about an inch long. To help prevent infection, paint the end of the cord with iodine.

Take the puppies and the mother to your veterinarian one to two days after delivery so he or she can make sure the puppies are healthy and the mother has sufficient milk and has not retained any afterbirth (placenta). The puppy's dewclaws, if present, are usually removed at this time.

Care of the Puppies

When the puppies are born make sure your Lhasa has milk and the puppies are nursing. The first milk the mother secretes is called colostrum. Colostrum contains antibodies produced by the mother that protect the puppies against diseases the mother is resistant to. It is very important the puppies receive this colostrum since they are unable to make these antibodies for themselves until they are older.

Breeding Lhasas

A female Lhasa nursing her hungry puppies. Lhasa mothers are usually very attentive to the needs of their young.

Check the puppies to be certain they are all getting enough milk. A healthy puppy is warm, content, and naps frequently. They seldom whimper and steadily gain weight. An underfed puppy is restless, thin, cool to the touch, and cries frequently, voicing its displeasure. Puppies grow and develop rapidly. At approximately two weeks of age, their eyes will open and they'll get their first glimpse of the world around them. It's exciting to observe each puppy explore its surroundings and begin to develop its own unique personality.

You may be called upon to feed a weak puppy or raise an entire litter if, for example, the mother does not produce enough milk. Or sometimes a very young mother will refuse to let her puppies nurse. In any case, here are some tips to rearing the puppies until they can be weaned.

First, it's imperative the puppies be kept warm. Newborn puppies can't regulate their own body temperature very well until they are at least two weeks old. Their environmental temperature should be maintained between 85°–90°F (29.4°–32.2°C) for the first two weeks of their life and then can be tapered down to 75°F (23.9°C) by the fourth week. Placing a heating pad under one-half of the puppy's bedding allows the puppies themselves to choose the amount of heat they desire to stay comfortable. Remember, overheating can be harmful too. The best way to know if the correct temperature is being maintained is to place an outdoor thermometer in the bed and monitor the temperature. Of course, if the mother is unable to nurse, the next step will be to feed your little charges. Commercial canine milk replacement formulas such as Esbilac are excellent. They can be purchased from your veterinarian or pet store. In an emergency you can make your own formula by mixing 3 egg yolks in 1 cup of milk.

A medicine dropper or small nursing bottle can be used to feed the formula to the puppies. Warm the milk to 95°–100°F (35°–37.8°C) prior to feeding. How much and how often to feed depends on how large the puppies are and how easily they consume the formula. Generally puppies will tell you when they're full by refusing to nurse anymore. If their little bellies are rounded and they're not crying they have probably had enough. A newborn needs to be fed about every four hours. As the puppies grow

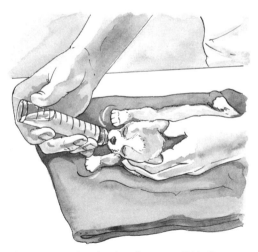

Pet nursers and canine formulas are available from pet stores or your veterinarian. Bottle feeding can save a puppy's life in the event it is unable to nurse or is not getting enough milk from its mother.

stronger the feeding can be reduced to every six to eight hours.

If the mother is able to clean the puppies, let her do so. If not, you'll have to stimulate their urinating and defecation. You can simulate the mother's licking by massaging the abdomen and genital area with a warm cotton ball. As the puppies grow the demands on the mother's milk production increase dramatically. To keep up, it's not unusual for the mother to double or even triple her food intake. To insure adequate intake, feed her two or three times daily. Adding some meat to the diet may also be needed to increase consumption.

Weaning

Under most circumstances weaning can take place when the puppies reach four to six weeks of age. You may begin the weaning process by offering small amounts of gruel when the puppies are three to four weeks old. The easiest way to prepare the gruel is to moisten dry or canned puppy food with water or milk until it has the consistency of thick soup. Using a commercial puppy food has the advantage of providing complete nutrition and gets the puppies used to their normal ration at an early age. Giving the puppies lots of table foods may encourage them to be finicky as adults. Four feedings per day is sufficient. To entice the puppies to eat solid food, try hand feeding them by letting them lick food off your fingers. I wouldn't advise leaving bowls of food and water in their whelping box. The water bowl will be mistaken for a wading pool and they'll be wearing more food than they could possibly consume. Gradually, over a two to three-week period thicken the feeding mixture until it is semisolid. The puppies' mother will appreciate your efforts to wean the puppies. Don't be surprised if the mother looks a little ragged by the time the pups are ready to be weaned. All her efforts have been directed toward caring for the puppies and providing enough milk. This extracts a toll from the moth-

er's body. Fortunately, it's only a temporary condition, and soon after weaning the mother's coat and overall condition will improve markedly. To facilitate weaning, separate the puppies from their mother, gradually lengthening the time they are apart. The less the mother is allowed to nurse, the less interested she'll be in nursing the puppies. To help prevent your Lhasa from becoming engorged with milk at weaning time, decrease her feed intake. If she eats less, she'll produce less milk. When the puppies are not allowed to nurse it's normal for the mother's breasts to be swollen and slightly sensitive. This should only last a day or two.

If any time during the nursing or weaning period the mother's breasts become hard, red, and hot to the touch call your veterinarian. She may have a case of mastitis which is inflammation and infection of the breast tissue.

The Puppies' Social Development

One of the most remarkable and enjoyable aspects of raising a litter of puppies is observing their rapid physical and social development. In humans the changes that occur from infant to toddler to adolescent take years while dogs accomplish the transition from newborn, helpless puppies to adult, independent dogs in a matter of months. Puppies exhibit an incremental, predictable pattern of socialization that coincides with their simultaneously developing motor skills and nervous system. The interaction a puppy experiences with its mother, littermates, and human beings the first weeks of its life are crucial for the puppy to develop normal adult behavioral characteristics. Studies have shown that puppies reared together without human contact until they were twelve weeks old were afraid of humans and many were untrainable. Puppies denied human contact their first four weeks of life, then given human interaction from four to ten weeks of age developed normal, healthy relationships with humans.

Breeding Lhasas

There are four recognized phases associated with a puppy's behavioral and social development. They are the neonatal period, the transition period, the socialization period, and the juvenile period. Understanding the changes puppies go through during these four phases will help you evaluate each puppy's development. It's important to get puppies started out correctly because their social development as puppies can shape their behavior for the rest of their lives.

The Neonatal Period occurs during the first two weeks of a puppy's life. Blind and deaf at birth, the newborn puppy is completely dependent on its mother. The neonate relies on a good sense of smell and touch to accomplish its main goals, i.e., to stay close to its mother and locate her nipples for the nourishment needed to survive. Social behavior with its littermates is minimal. Crawling, suckling, and crying when distressed are the newborn's major motor activities. Life is pretty simple for puppies at this age. They eat, sleep, and stay close to their mother for warmth because newborn puppies don't have the ability to regulate their own body temperature very well. Even evacuation of the neonate's bowels and urination requires stimulation by the mother. Communication by the newborn puppies consists of whimpering and crying to get their mother's attention when they are cold or hungry.

During the transition period remarkable transformations take place between the puppies' second and third weeks of age. Their motor skills have progressed to the point where they are no longer helpless little creatures. They can stand, walk, and chew and are no longer completely dependent on their mother. They are able to eliminate without the mother's help now, and will even do so outside the nesting area. The newborn's world now includes sights and smells because eyes open and ears begin to function during this time. Early signs of social behavior can be observed. This is when a puppy will begin to acknowledge people and may even wag its tail at the sight of a human being or the sound of a voice. Playing with littermates also begins during this phase of development.

The socialization period lasts from about the fourth to the twelfth week of a puppy's life. This is the most important two months of a dog's life in terms of social and behavioral development. The knowledge and behavior acquired during this time lays the foundation for subsequent adult relationships with other dogs and human beings.

Early in this period the puppy's major concerns are the necessities of life—namely food, warmth, and security. The puppy naturally forms a very strong attachment to its mother, and will try to follow her everywhere she goes. Puppies are not very secure without their mother at this time and will cry if they feel isolated or alone. By the fourth and fifth week littermates are vigorously playing with each other and not always on friendly terms! In fact this is the time when competitive behavior between littermates can be observed. They'll be jostling for attention and establishing a social hierarchy among themselves. At around five weeks of age you'll be able to recognize which puppies will be dominant and outgoing individuals and which puppies will be the timid and submissive ones. By five to six weeks of age the puppies are starting to venture out of the nest on their own and explore their environment. Pack behavior is observed at this time. One puppy will take the bold initiative and begin to wander around and the other littermates will tag along. As the puppy matures at this time it will eliminate farther away from the nest; elimination behavior is being formed at this time. Housebreaking is much easier if it begins at an early age (six to eight weeks of age), before bad habits are learned. Puppies are also weaned from their mother during this socialization period, usually around six weeks of age. Teeth are erupting, enabling the puppies to eat solid food. Chewing becomes a major activity, as anyone with a puppy will testify. Weaning also serves to break the emotional umbilical cord to the mother; puppies become noticeably more independent when they reach this milestone.

The relative independence the puppy enjoys at

Breeding Lhasas

about six weeks of age paves the way for more complex social interactions with humans. Human contact is very important between the puppy's sixth to eighth week of life and the puppies in turn are very responsive to human interaction. It is especially at this time that puppies need to be handled, talked to, played with, and given generous doses of love and affection. Lots of human contact at this age will pay big dividends for the rest of the puppy's life. This is why eight-week-old puppies are at a good age to be placed in their new homes. The bond between the puppy and its new owner forms rapidly at this time.

The Juvenile Period extends from the puppy's twelfth week of age until it reaches sexual maturity. This is when young dogs must learn to fit into their new household. Some dogs may test their owners during this time and may even attempt to achieve dominance of the household. Some Lhasa apsos, particularly males, are strong-willed and may test their new owner. New dog owners need to understand that this is the age when many behavior problems arise if the dog is not trained and supervised properly. Of course any puppy at this age is bound to get into mischief and try its owner's patience from time to time. This goes with the territory of owning a new puppy. Try to anticipate problems before they end up causing lots of aggravation. For example, if the new puppy likes to chew, don't leave him in the living room unattended for very long. You'll be asking for trouble if you do, because he'll probably pick the most valuable piece of furniture in the room to chew on!

Lhasa apsos come in a variety of colors and combinations to suit almost everyone's fancy. Some owners prefer to clip the hair around the eyes or pull the hair back and secure it with a barrette or rubber band.

Understanding Lhasa Apsos

History of the Breed

The origins of the Lhasa apso can be traced to the exotic and mysterious mountain land known as Tibet. Nestled high in the Himalayan mountains north of India and Nepal, Tibet is now part of China. Home of Mt. Everest, the towering Himalayan mountains kept Tibet isolated from much of the world for centuries. Exotic tales of Tibetan myths and rituals have always intrigued Westerners. The Lhasa apso is firmly rooted in Tibetan folklore and culture. Lhasas have probably existed in Tibet for 800 years, although it is only in this century that the rest of the world has been introduced to the breed.

For hundreds of years it was customary for the Dalai Lamas (Tibetan leaders) to bestow the Lhasa apso as a gift to visiting dignitaries from China and other neighboring lands. To receive a Lhasa was considered to be a great honor and it was thought to bring good luck to the recipient. Legend has it Lhasas were involved in religious ceremonies and considered sacred because the souls of deceased Dalai Lamas were thought to enter the bodies of Lhasa apsos.

Inside the aristocratic Tibetan household the Lhasa apso was used as a sentinel dog. The large, imposing Tibetan mastiff was employed outside to physically intimidate and ward off any intruders, but the shaggy little Lhasa was relied on to sound the alarm to warn the house members of any danger. Through centuries of breeding, the Lhasa developed a keen instinct for being able to distinguish friend from foe. In native Tibetan language the Lhasa apso is known as "Abso Seng Kye," which means "Barking sentinel lion dog"!

The Lhasa apso is one of four breeds native to Tibet, the others being the Tibetan terrier, the Tibetan spaniel, and the huge Tibetan mastiff. All have thick, dense coats that are well suited to the harsh, frigid mountain climate. The Lhasa apso is named after Lhasa, the capital city of Tibet. Apso is thought to be derived from the Tibetan word "rapso" meaning "goatlike," owing to the breed's long, dense, shaggy coat. In some countries the Lhasa apso is referred to as the Tibetan apso.

It wasn't until the twentieth century that the Lhasa apso was introduced into England and the United States. Taikoo, a black and white male Lhasa, and Dinkie, a female the "color of raw silk," were the first Lhasa apsos to enter the United States. Around 1934, the Tibetan Breeds Association was formed to delineate the characteristics of the Tibetan breeds and to lay the foundation for establishing breed standards. The following year, 1935, the American Kennel Club officially adopted breed standards for the Lhasa apso. These breed standards have remained relatively unchanged. It wasn't until 1978 that any modifications were made in the standards and these were relatively minor changes.

Getting to Know Lhasa Apsos

There are many reasons Lhasa apsos have become popular pets. Several Lhasa owners I have talked to tell me they "fell in love" with the cutest little puppy they had ever seen! Their appearance alone makes them hard to resist as a soft, furry household pet. Unfortunately, many people purchase a dog based on appearance and emotion without giving much thought to the temperament, instincts, and behavioral characteristics commonly observed in the breed. The qualities that endear our

Above: There is no substitute for time and attention in developing a loving bond between a dog and its owner. Below: Grooming is an important aspect of Lhasa care. Lhasas that receive lots of attention generally will enjoy being brushed.

Understanding Lhasa Apsos

canine friends to us, such as companionship and loyalty, come from within each dog's own unique psychological makeup. No matter how beautiful its physical appearance, a dog will not be a very enjoyable pet if it can't be trained or is aggressive and bites its owners.

Lhasa apsos have made ideal pets for many of my clients. The Lhasa's natural instinct is to be wary of strangers. Many single or retired people I know enjoy the sense of security their Lhasas give them. A dog that barks when a stranger approaches the house is a good deterrent to crime. The dog

Parts of a Lhasa Apso.
1. ears 2. skull 3. stop 4. cheek 5. muzzle 6. shoulder 7. chest 8. brisket 9. forequarters 10. front pastern 11. ribcage 12. stifle 13. hindquarters 14. hock 15. rear pastern 16. loin 17. tail 18. withers 19. neckline

Understanding Lhasa Apsos

needn't be large, it just needs to make noise. This fact reminds me of a program that appeared on convicted house burglars. The inmates interviewed said if they approached a house with a barking dog inside it was too risky to burglarize. They didn't need the extra hassle and besides, they added, there were plenty of other easy targets! So the bottom line here is don't let the small size of the Lhasa fool you. They are a hardy breed and loyal companions.

The Lhasa apso's relatively small size can be a real asset. Tipping the scales at 15 to 25 pounds, the Lhasa can easily be picked up and carried. Since they don't require large amounts of space, Lhasas make ideal pets for living primarily inside the home. This is especially appealing for those whose yard space is limited, such as apartment or condominium dwellers. Living in the city will suit your Lhasa just fine. Remember, for hundreds of generations Lhasas were bred to live within the confines of the aristocratic Tibetan household.

Very few breeds can match the Lhasa apso's color variations. There is a color to suit almost everyone's fancy. Black, white, black and white, honey, brown, slate, smoke, and many combinations thereof constitute some of the colors one can expect to find in the Lhasa apso. The long, dense coat of the Lhasa is, of course, a hallmark of the breed and gives it an air of nobility. A well-groomed Lhasa is a beautiful sight to behold and many Lhasa owners take great pride in the appearance of their dog and rightly so, because it can take a considerable amount of time to keep a Lhasa well-groomed. This is an important point that prospective Lhasa owners should carefully consider. It is absolutely essential to keep their coats free of mats. More than just a cosmetic concern, a Lhasa with a mass of matted hair will be much more likely to have skin infections, harbor fleas, and be generally uncomfortable. Many Lhasa owners opt to leave the grooming in the hands of a professional groomer. This is a wise choice if you are not able to commit the proper amount of time needed to keep your Lhasa's coat in top form.

As is the case with any breed that has become

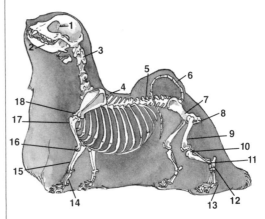

The skeletal system of a Lhasa Apso.
1. skull (cranium) 2. lower jaw (mandible) 3. cervical vertebrae 4. thoracic vertebrae 5. lumbar vertebrae 6. tail vertebrae 7. pelvis 8. hip joint 9. femur 10. knee joint (stifle) 11. tibia and fibula 12. hock (tarsas) 13. metatarsals 14. metacarpals 15. radius and ulna 16. elbow 17. humerus 18. shoulder joint

fashionable, purchasing just any pure-breed Lhasa apso is no guarantee you'll be receiving a top-quality dog. Less-than-scrupulous breeders are more than willing to take advantage of the public's demand for popular dogs by producing inferior, genetically weak dogs with poor dispositions. And who's to tell the difference? On an unsuspecting public, it is not that difficult to pass off these low-quality dogs when they are cute little puppies. It's not until the puppies reach maturity that someone realizes their dream puppy is turning into a nightmare of behavioral problems and veterinary bills! The bottom line here is, know what you're getting before you buy. Take the time to find breeders or pet stores that enjoy good reputations and take a genuine interest in the breed. I can tell you from experience with many pet owners, a dog that was initially a ''bargain'' may not be such a bargain in the long run if it does not meet your expectations.

Understanding Lhasa Apsos

Underneath all that hair is a well-developed muscular system. Lhasa Apsos are agile and strong in relation to their size.

It's no wonder the Lhasa apso has become a popular breed. The world-wide tendency toward urbanization has created a niche for the Lhasa apso, yet it is a breed hardy enough to thrive in almost any climate and environment.

The Lhasa apso is a dog that loves to be pampered yet it is pugnacious enough to hold its own against foes many times its size. For companionship and loyalty it's hard to beat the Lhasa apso.

AKC Lhasa Apso Breed Standard

The following is the American Kennel Club Lhasa Apso breed standard. The original standard was adopted April 9, 1935, and has been revised only once. The changes in the standard were relatively minor. The revised standard was approved July 11, 1978.

Character: Gay and assertive, but chary of strangers.

Size: Variable but about 10 inches (25.4 cm) or 11 inches (27.9 cm) at shoulder for dogs; bitches slightly smaller.

Color: All colors equally acceptable with or without dark tips to ears and beard.

Body Shape: The length from point of shoulders to point of buttocks longer than height at withers, well ribbed up, strong loin, well-developed quarters and thighs.

Coat: Heavy, straight, hard, not wooly nor silky, of good length, and very dense.

Mouth and Muzzle: The preferred bite is either level or slightly undershot. Muzzle of medium length; a square muzzle is objectionable.

Head: Heavy head furnishings with good fall over eyes, good whiskers and beard; skull narrow, falling away behind the eyes in a marked degree, not quite flat, but not domed or apple-shaped; straight foreface of fair length. Nose black, the length from tip of nose to eye to be roughly one-third of the total length from nose to back of skull.

Eyes: Dark brown, neither very large and full, nor very small and sunk.

Ears: Pendant, heavily feathered.

Legs: Forelegs straight; both forelegs and hind legs heavily furnished with hair.

Feet: Well feathered, should be round and cat-like, with good pads.

Tail and Carriage: Well feathered, should be carried well over back in a screw, there may be a kink at the end. A low carriage of stern is a serious fault.

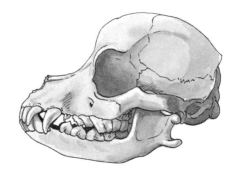

A Lhasa's head should be slightly rounded but not dome shaped. Note the shortened muzzle. That is characteristic of Lhasas.

Useful Addresses and Literature

International Kennel Clubs

American Lhasa Apso Club*
  Lynette Clooney, Secretary
  25 Ranco Dr. N.
  Keller, Texas 76248
American Kennel Club
  51 Madison Avenue
  New York, NY 10038
Australian National Kennel Club
  Royal Show Grounds
  Ascot Vale
  Victoria
  Australia
Canadian Kennel Club
  111 Eglington Avenue
  Toronto 12, Ontario
  Canada
Irish Kennel Club
  41 Harcourt Street
  Dublin 2
  Ireland
The Kennel Club
  1–4 Clargis Street
  Picadilly
  London, W7Y 8AB
  England
New Zealand Kennel Club
  P.O. Box 523
  Wellington
  New Zealand

* This address may change as a new officer is elected. The latest listing can always be obtained from the American Kennel Club.

Books

Alderton, David *The Dog Care Manual.* Barron's Educational Series, Hauppauge, New York, 1986.

Baer, Ted *Communicating with Your Dog.* Barron's Educational Series, Hauppauge, New York, 1984.

Frye, Fredric L. *First Aid for Your Dog.* Barron's Educational Series, Hauppauge, New York, 1987.

Klever, Ulrich *The Complete Book of Dog Care.* Barron's Educational Series, Hauppauge, New York, 1984.

Lorenz, Konrad Z. *Man Meets Dog.* Penguin Books, London and New York, 1967.

Nieburg, Herbert, A. and Arlene Fischer *Pet Loss: A Thoughtful Guide for Adults and Children.* Harper and Row, New York, 1982.

Quackenbush, James, E. and D. Graveline *When Your Pet Dies: How to Cope with Your Feelings.* Simon and Schuster, New York, 1985.

Rosenberg, Marc, A. *Companion Animal Loss and Pet Owner Grief.* ALPO Center, 1985. Library of Congress Catalog Card Number 85-73830.

Ullman, Hans-J. *The New Dog Handbook.* Barron's Educational Series, Hauppauge, New York, 1984.

Pet Loss and Human Emotion. American Veterinary Medical Association, 930 North Meacham Road, Schaumberg, Illinois 60196. (Free)

Touring with Towser: a directory of hotels and motels that accommodate guests with dogs. Gaines TWT, P.O. Box 8172, Kankakee, Illinois 60901 (price: $1.50).

White, Betty. *Pet Love.* Morrow, New York, 1983.

Index

Index